MW01060625

SEW

A Beginner's
Guide to Sewing
20 Chic Projects

TAMMY JOHAL

SIMPLE

Photography by Emily Lavarello

Quadrille

CONTENTS

06	Introduction
08	How to use this book
10	Tools you'll need
14	Terms & techniques
18	How to pick your fabric
20	How to measure your body to pick a size
22	Using patterns
24	How to print & assemble a digital pattern
26	How to grade a pattern
27	Basic pattern adjustments
32	Have you sewn something & you now hate it?
35	How to cut your fabric

36 CORE SEWING TECHNIQUES

38	How to sew a seam
40	How to finish a seam
43	Common sewing problems
44	How to sew on buttons
46	How to add pockets to any pattern in this book
50	How to shirr fabric
52	How to gather fabric
54	How to attach knit binding/bands
56	How to sew skinny straps
58	How to sew a dart
60	How to sew a side slit

62 THE PATTERNS

64	Scrunchie
68	Tie Tote Bag
74	Maxi Skirt
82	Trendy Tote Bag
86	Shirred Dress & Top
96	Camisole Top & Dress
104	Button-back Top
112	Halter-neck Dress & Top
120	Tie-front Top
130	Cover-up & Light Summer Jacket
138	Cut-out Dress
148	Stretch Midi Skirt
156	Drawstring Trousers & Shorts
168	Tank Top
176	Button-front Dress

188	Index
190	About the Author
191	Acknowledgements

PAGE 82

PAGE 130

PAGE 176

PAGE 74

PAGE 96

PAGE 86

PAGE 112

PAGE 156

PAGE 64

PAGE 120

PAGE 138

PAGE 68

PAGE 104

PAGE 148

PAGE 168

INTRODUCTION

Sewing will be the best skill you'll ever learn...
I know it has been for me, so I'm here to introduce
you to this wonderful, fabric-filled world. Whether
you've never turned on a sewing machine before
or you've completed a couple of projects over
the years, this book will get you sewing garments
you'll feel proud of.

As a British Indian woman, I've always been surrounded by embellished, glamorous outfits. I have countless memories of my grandma designing our next Indian outfits and spending hours at the tailors getting the fit just right. It was my first glimpse into the sewing world and opened my eyes to how garments are sewn from pieces of fabric.

I remember the first thing I ever sewed was at primary school. It was a bright pink cotton skirt with a thick black waistband. It was fun learning how to sew it, but I never wore it and didn't turn on the machine after that. Why was that? I now realize it's because that skirt didn't actually reflect the clothes I wore or wanted to wear. It felt like I made something for the sake of it rather than something for me to wear and really be proud of.

Fast forward to 2018, when I decided to sew my own clothes again. But this time, I wanted to give it a proper go and make pieces that fit my wardrobe and got me excited to wear them. After sewing countless garments, I could never find the perfect patterns that truly captured the stylish and trendy look I was after. It frustrated me because I knew I wanted to learn how to sew but I didn't want to spend hours making something that would resemble my grandma's curtains. That's when I dedicated endless hours to learning how to draft my own patterns to create clothes I wanted to wear. Tammy Handmade sewing patterns was born and has allowed thousands of sewists across the globe to sew clothes that look modern and stylish.

I know you might be thinking you don't have endless hours free to dedicate to learning a new skill, but I promise you that you'll be able to make some of the projects in this book in one hour or less! Some of my best-selling sewing patterns can be sewn in under an hour and are staple pieces I reach for every day in my wardrobe. Sewing doesn't have to mean painstakingly hand-sewing every seam or creating super-complex garments. It can mean making clothes you'll want to wear and that you also enjoy making.

The majority of patterns in this book are simple to sew, and you'll be able to complete them in a couple of hours or one day max! I want you to create something you're truly proud of and be able to wear that evening. I hate fussing with tricky fastenings, so the garments in this book all have a slip-on style with no zips. The pieces you'll learn to create will not only become staples in your wardrobe that you'll want to wear over and over again but actually reflect the modern and stylish pieces you'll find in your favourite high-street shops. Try mixing and matching the garments to create your own handmade wardrobe and, hopefully, you'll do a double-take when you pass a mirror!

Sewing allows me to make clothes I truly love, and I hope to share that same ability with you.

Tammy xxx

HOW TO USE THIS BOOK

This book has 20 beginner-friendly sewing projects (15 projects plus five distinct variations) that will become wardrobe staples, whether you're new to sewing or a complete pro! You might feel an urge to get sewing straight away, but before you start, it's going to make the whole process so much easier if you take the time to read about all the different sewing tools, techniques and guidance first.

In the early part of the book, you'll learn the basics of sewing, from how to pick the perfect fabric, to how to measure your body and so much more to guide you every step of the way. Next, I'll explain various core sewing techniques. These will be the building blocks you'll use depending on which pattern you're going to sew. Try to familiarize yourself with these and practise on scrap pieces of fabric first. It's going to make it so much less intimidating when sewing your final garments because you've already practised the techniques you'll need!

Once you feel ready to tackle your first project, feel free to flip back to the beginning of this book to remind yourself of all the techniques you've learnt. I've always been someone who jumps straight into the deep end; it's how I personally learn best, so start by choosing a project that resonates with you and resembles what you want to make!

The patterns in this book range from super easy to intermediate and are designed so you can mix and match the pieces to create endless outfits. By the end of this book, I want you to be able to sew something you're proud of and walk around telling everyone 'I MADE THIS!' With your own hands, time and energy, you were able to create something from scratch and, in the process, learn the key foundations to making your own clothes.

QR code

Scan the above QR code to access the pattern downloads for this book. The patterns are available to download and print in A4/US letter or A0. See page 24 for instructions on how to print and assemble a digital pattern.

TOOLS YOU'LL NEED

There are a few absolute essentials that you'll need to start sewing your own clothes, and I've listed them below to help you on your journey. Some of these can range in price, so don't feel like you need to buy the most expensive equipment when you're first starting out. You'll need these for the projects in the book.

SEWING MACHINE

There are so many machines out there on the market, but at a bare minimum all you need is one that can sew a straight stitch and a zigzag stitch. My first machine was the cheapest I could find, and it helped me develop a love for this skill and got me through learning all the basics of sewing. If you're someone that loves technology and having a machine that feels like a cool gadget, then you might want to look into a computerized machine. These digital types of machines really simplify the sewing process and can make it much easier to learn as a beginner.

SEWING-MACHINE NEEDLES

There are lots of sewing-machine needles out there for you to try, but to start out with, find a pack of Universal needles and Ballpoint needles.

Universal needles can be used for lots of types of projects and if you buy a pack, you'll notice there are different sizes depending on what fabric you're sewing with. You'll also need to double check that the needles you buy fit your sewing machine – most needles will specify which brands or machines they suit.

Ballpoint needles have a rounded point and are perfect for sewing with stretch fabric. If you use a Universal needle on stretch fabric it may tear the fabric or leave skipped stitches, so make sure to get a pack of both these needle types.

THREAD

Thread can make or break a sewing project, literally! You'll want to get in the habit of using high-quality thread because cheaper ones can snap very easily. You can find great all-purpose thread made out of cotton or polyester and these can be used on all types of sewing projects. When I first started sewing, I just bought a pack of thread containing 20 different colours, which is more than enough to start making clothes as we want the thread to roughly match what we're sewing.

SCISSORS

You can't just use your kitchen scissors to cut fabric because you want to be able to achieve sharp, clean cuts. Invest in a pair of good-quality dressmaking scissors/ shears so all your cutting will be much more precise and efficient. I also recommend buying a separate pair of ordinary scissors to cut your paper pattern pieces, this is because paper can dull the blades over time. Cutting out your fabric precisely is one of the most important steps in sewing, so take your time to find ones you love. In addition, a small pair of scissors or some thread snips will be useful to keep by your sewing machine to cut thread ends.

PINS & CLIPS

Both pins and clips are really useful tools to help you hold fabric together. Pins come in different lengths, styles and materials but I prefer using glass-headed ones because you can iron over them. Now to save you the headache I had for years, I 100% recommend getting a magnetic pin cushion because once you knock those pins on the floor it will be a nightmare to pick them all up again without one of these. Clips are super useful if you find pins too tricky and small to hold or when dealing with thick layers. I love using clips instead of pins in most of my sewing but it's great to have both!

SAFETY PINS

You'll probably have several of these lying around in a random drawer, so try to gather a handful to keep in your sewing collection. These are useful for fitting instead of using pins, but they're also used in several projects in this book for threading cord or elastic through channels.

MEASURING TAPE

Not only does one of these look cool dangling from your neck, but a measuring tape is also an essential tool for accurately measuring your body. You'll need a flexible one that can bend around your body and easily measure curved areas. Many of them are made out of flexible cloth, plastic or fibreglass to prevent them from tearing or stretching.

RULER

You'll want a ruler to measure the 1in (2.5cm) square box on your digital pattern to check the size is correct, and one will also come in handy for measuring or checking the width of seam allowances and hems.

SEAM RIPPER

Making mistakes is part of the process of learning and to help you fix them you'll need a seam ripper. This is a small tool that gently cuts the thread on a seam you've just sewn without tearing the fabric. If you realize you've sewn two wrong pieces together, simply use this to unpick the thread easily and pick up where you left off. You'll also want a seam ripper when you get around to making buttonholes, as once you've stitched these, you'll need one to open up the gap in the middle.

IRON

Pressing your seams once sewn is the easiest way to make your garments look professionally made. You'll want to invest in a good-quality iron that also has a steam function, as well as an ironing board. Once you sew a seam it rarely lies flat on its own – you'll need to press it with an iron to achieve a clean, crisp look. Along with the iron, I'd also advise that you get a pressing cloth to protect delicate fabrics and stretch fabrics like jersey.

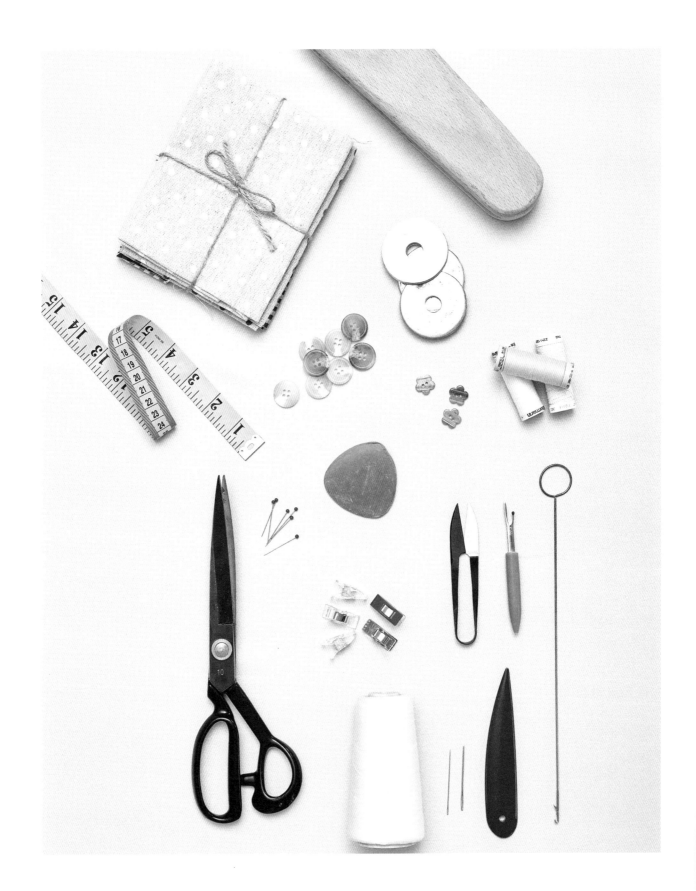

NICE TO HAVES

FABRIC MARKERS

Fabric markers such as pens or chalk are super useful when transferring pattern markings and details onto your fabric. If you try using a standard pencil or pen, the markings will be permanent and might not show up on darker fabrics. However, chalk or water-erasable pens will show up on most fabrics and disappear in the wash or once steamed. I also like to use fabric pens to mark the wrong side of the fabric if it's hard to tell which side is which by eye.

HAND-SEWING NEEDLES

It's always useful to have a pack of hand-sewing needles in your kit! As well as being useful for sewing seams or hems by hand, they're perfect for sewing on buttons and even tucking away raw overlocker threads inside. They come in various sizes and thicknesses, allowing you to use the perfect one for your project. Because they're small and easy to carry around, a pack of mixed needles is great for quick fixes when out and about!

LOOP TURNER/TURNING SET

If you're going to be making skinny (shoestring/spaghetti) straps, a loop turner or turning set will be invaluable. Yes, you can turn these thin fabric tubes out by laboriously poking the fabric through with something like a chopstick or use a safety pin, but the proper tools will speed things up dramatically. A loop turner is basically a long thin latched hook that you insert into the fabric tube to grab the far end so you can gradually ease it out. With a turning set you get a set of stiff tubes and corresponding rods in different sizes. You insert the appropriate tube into your tube of fabric and then use the rod to push from the closed end of the fabric tube. The fabric slides through the stiff tube and is easily turned out.

OVERLOCKER/SERGER

In addition to a sewing machine, you can also purchase an overlocker. This type of machine is perfect for sewing stretch fabrics and neatly finishing the raw edges on woven fabrics. I didn't buy an overlocker until one year into my sewing journey and now I can't imagine not having it!

PATTERN WEIGHTS

As an alternative to using pins when cutting out your pattern pieces, you can use weights. You can buy these or you can simply use washers or other items you have around the house to weigh your patterns down while you cut around them.

PINKING SHEARS

If you don't have an overlocker and don't want to use a zigzag stitch on your sewing machine to finish raw edges, then try using pinking shears! These serrated scissors are used to finish raw edges to help prevent fraying on woven fabrics. It's a quick-and-easy method and is great for reducing seam bulk at curved edges.

ROTARY CUTTER & CUTTING MAT

If you find you are doing a lot of sewing, or if you find you can't cut as accurately as you'd like with scissors, you may wish to invest in a rotary cutter and cutting mat. For dressmaking you'll want a large cutting mat so you can cut a good portion of a pattern out before you need to move the fabric or mat to cut the next section. Don't be tempted to skip on the cutting mat as without one you'll cut grooves in your table and blunt the cutting wheel quite quickly!

TAILOR'S CLAPPER

I didn't purchase one of these until a few years into my sewing journey and wow, I missed out! A tailor's clapper is a wooden tool that helps achieve flat, even seams with the help of your iron. After sewing a seam, you press it with an iron and lots of steam and then firmly press down with your tailor's clapper to lock everything in place. The pressure of pressing down combined with the steam creates a crisp finish. It's also really useful if the fabric you're using is spongy and won't press with just an iron.

TERMS & TECHNIQUES

This is the how-to section where you'll find information on selecting your fabric, measuring your body, printing and adjusting your pattern plus how to use a pattern in order to get sewing. But first, let's start with an explanation of terms.

GLOSSARY OF SEWING TERMS

Sewing instructions are filled with terminology that you might not have heard before. It can be daunting opening up a pattern and not knowing what on earth all these words mean, so I've put together this handy guide of key words and phrases for you. These are the most commonly used terms that you'll come across time and time again.

Backstitch: At the beginning and end of a seam sewn on your sewing machine, you should sew back and forth a few stitches to prevent the seam from unravelling. This is also known as a reverse stitch or a back tack.

Baste/tack: Before sewing a seam, it can be useful to baste the pieces of fabric together, especially when dealing with curves. This is where you sew your fabric pieces together using a long stitch length to hold the layers in place temporarily. You can either do this on your sewing machine or by hand using a needle. Once you've sewn your final seam, use a seam ripper to remove the temporary basting stitch.

Binding: To finish raw fabric edges, you can use binding, which is a narrow strip of fabric. Commercial binding is cut on the fabric bias which gives it some stretch to enable it to bend smoothly around curves and angles. The binding encases the raw edges and can be used on woven or knit fabrics.

Bodice: Instructions often refer to the bodice piece, which is the section covering the torso. There can be a front and back bodice for tops, dresses and shirts etc.

Clip: Using scissors, make a small cut into the seam allowance. Useful after sewing curved edges such as a neckline or armhole as it helps allow the garment to sit flat.

Dart: A dart is sewn into fabric to contour the shape at areas such as the bust or waist. It is usually triangular (although you can get diamond-shaped or curved darts) and you join the fabric along the two long edges of the dart to give the fabric a three-dimensional shape.

Drape: Fabric can vary drastically from stiff and paper-like to soft and floppy, so it's useful to understand the drape of the material. Drape is the way the fabric looks and behaves when it's hanging off the body. A fabric such as satin will have a fluid and loose drape because it will move easily and freely, while a fabric such as linen will have a stiffer drape that moves more rigidly. If you're trying to sew a flowy dress, it's important to use a lightweight fabric that has a fluid drape.

Ease: If you try on a garment from your own wardrobe, you might notice it's not skin tight. There might be an extra inch (2.5cm) or so around the bust and/or waist to give you room to breathe, move and put it on easily. This is called 'ease' in sewing terms. Garments will have different amounts of ease which will determine how fitted or loose your garment will be after it is sewn.

Facing: To finish off areas such as a neckline or armholes, you can use a facing which is a separate piece of fabric. Don't worry, it won't be visible: you can sew the facing to the garment neckline and then roll it inside so it's neatly finished and hidden from the outside.

Finish seams: Once you've sewn a seam, you'll want to neaten the raw edges to prevent fraying, add stability and increase durability. This is known as finishing the seams. There are many ways to do this on your sewing machine, overlocker or using pinking shears. If I'm sewing with woven fabrics, I tend to use my overlocker to neatly finish the seam. If you want to use a sewing machine, you can use a zigzag stitch close to the edge to prevent it from fraying, or your machine might have an overcast stitch for this purpose. When sewing knit fabrics, you won't need to finish the seams as the raw edges won't fray!

Gather: Many summer skirts and dresses use a sewing technique called gathering. It's where fabric is bunched up into tiny neat folds by first stitching one or two lines of long straight stitches and then pulling up the sewing thread to draw the fabric in. The gathered fabric is then attached to another piece of fabric such as a dress bodice or waistband. Gathering is also sometimes used at the top of a sleeve.

Grade pattern: Sewing patterns are made for standard body measurements and don't take into account your unique shape. Maybe you've noticed when you look at a size chart your bust puts you into a size 12 but your waist puts you into a size 16. To help adjust the pattern to your body, you'll want to draw a line connecting both sizes at the desired points (see pages 26–31). This technique is called grading the pattern and allows you to fit patterns to your personal body shape.

Grade seam: To help reduce bulky seams, you can grade the seam. This isn't like a school grade! It involves using scissors to trim the seam allowances down to different widths and will result in a smoother finish.

Grainline: You can't just cut your pattern pieces out wherever they fit on the fabric (even if you are using a plain fabric) as how they are positioned relative to the fabric grain will affect how they hang. The grain on the fabric runs parallel to the selvedges/selvages and each pattern piece will have a double-headed arrow that should be lined up with the fabric grain before it is cut out (see page 23).

Hem: This is used to finish the edges of a garment that aren't stitched to any other fabric piece, such as the bottom of a sleeve or skirt. This is where the edge is folded once or twice and stitched close to the edge to neatly finish it. There are various ways to stitch your hem, but the simplest option is to fold the edge to the wrong side once or twice and then topstitch close to the fold, which is what I shall be doing for the projects in this book.

Interfacing: To make fabric more stable you can apply interfacing. This is a material that can be sewn or fused onto the wrong side of the fabric, depending on the type of interfacing you are using. I always prefer using interfacing that is fusible, which is where one side has glue on it. You simply use an iron to fuse it in place and once pressed it will stick to the fabric. Interfacing is useful for preventing stretching, for stabilizing areas and adding structure. You'll be able to find lots of weights and colours to add more or less structure depending on the garment you're sewing.

Lining: Garments sometimes have an extra fabric layer inside and this is called the lining. It helps provide a neat and clean finish inside and hides raw edges.

Notch: To help align your pattern pieces when sewing, you might have noticed there are short lines marked at the edges of pattern pieces. These are notches which can be marked on the fabric or cut into your fabric seam allowance. When pinning two notched edges together, match the notches first and then pin the rest of the seam, easing the fabric around curves if needed.

Pattern: A pattern is a template for a piece you need to cut out to make a specific item, but it is also a group term given to all the pieces you need as well as the instructions on how to sew the specific garment.

Pin: To help hold a seam together before you sew, you can use pins to keep everything in place. If you're dealing with heavy fabric or thick layers or if you find it difficult to hold pins, try using clips instead.

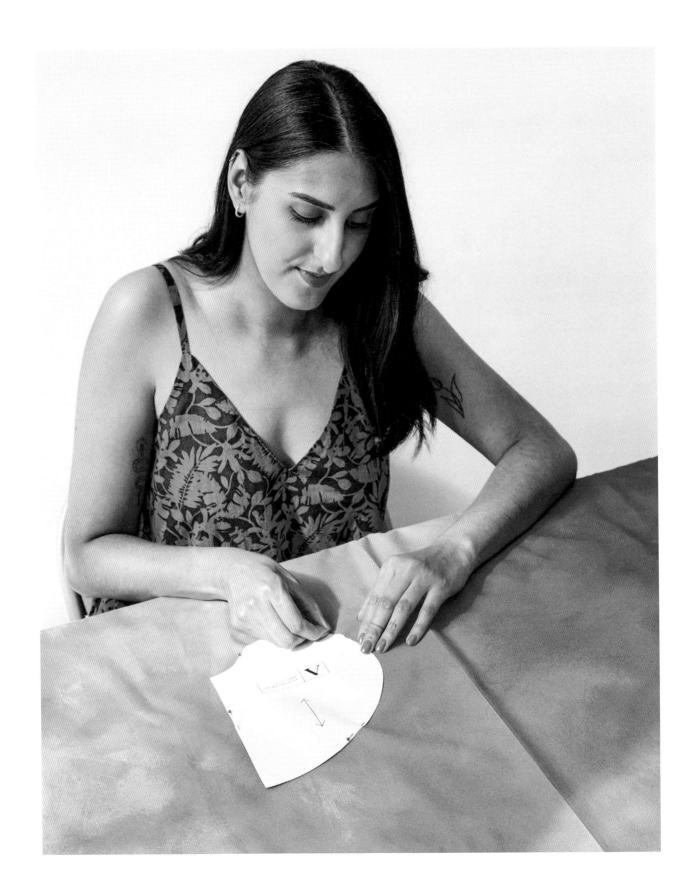

Right side: When cutting out and assembling your garment, it's important to know the 'right side' of the fabric. This is the pretty side that will be visible on the outside once sewn. I mark mine with chalk to make sure I am cutting pattern pieces correctly. Some fabrics might not have an obvious right side so you can use either side – just make sure you use the same fabric side for each piece! (The other side of the fabric is called the 'wrong side'.)

Right sides together: When sewing a seam, you will generally place two pieces of fabric together with the right sides facing each other. This will mean that once the seams are sewn the pretty sides are neatly finished and the raw seam edges are on the wrong side/inside of the garment.

Seam: To attach two pieces of material together, you sew a seam – a stitching line that joins both fabric pieces. There are various types of seam constructions which you can find on pages 38–42.

Seam allowance: This is the area in between the fabric raw edge and the stitching line. Seam allowances vary by garment and designer but in this book you'll be using ⅜in (1cm) seam allowances. It's important to remain precise when sewing and make sure your seam allowances are even and neatly sewn.

Selvedge/selvage: When you purchase fabric, you might notice there are two sides that look neatly finished. These are the selvedges/selvages, which are the finished edges on the long sides of the fabric when it is woven. Sometimes manufacturers include information on the selvedges, such as the brand, collection name and colour information. These edges won't fray but it's best not to include them when you cut your fabric pieces (even if they will be in a seam allowance) as they can be stiff and may not shrink at the same rate as the rest of the fabric.

Size chart: This is a table that lists the body measurements of each size you can sew for a pattern. This information helps you to choose the correct size as you can compare the chart against your own measurements. It's important also to look at the chart listing the finished garment measurements, so you can see the amount of ease included and how the garment will fit you. Size charts vary, so always take a moment to look at them before cutting out your pattern pieces.

Staystitch: To help prevent fabric from stretching out at key areas that are highly likely to stretch as you sew, such as a neckline, you can sew a line of straight stitches known as staystitching. This is sewn within the seam allowance so it won't be visible once the garment has been fully sewn.

Stitch in the ditch: Garments can be constructed with many layers and to help prevent anything from rolling to the right side, you can stitch along an existing seamline on the right side of the garment to keep things in place. This technique is known as stitching in the ditch.

Tack: See baste/tack.

Toile: Also sometimes called a muslin, this is a prototype of your garment that is sewn in cheaper fabric to test the fit. It's always best to make one of these for every sewing pattern you try so that you can get the fit right before cutting into your final fabric. It's also a useful step to help you understand the construction of the garment.

Topstitch: You can finish garment seams and edges with stitches that are visible from the outside. This is known as topstitching and can be purely decorative or it can have a function, such as adding stability or preventing linings or facings from rolling out.

Understitch: This is a useful technique to prevent linings or facings from rolling to the right side. Once you've sewn the facing to the garment, press the seam allowances towards the facing, then sew close to the seam line through the facing and seam allowances (but not the main part of the garment). Once you press the facing to the inside of the garment, the seam is naturally pulled to that side, making it (and the facing) invisible from the right side. This works best on light to medium-weight fabrics.

Wrong side: If you've already determined the right side of the fabric, the wrong side will be the other side. Sometimes it can be tricky to figure out but usually the wrong side will look more faded and dull.

HOW TO PICK YOUR FABRIC

Shopping for fabric has become a hobby I actually enjoy! The options are endless, and in this section, you'll learn how to choose the right fabric for your project.

I know it might sound simple, but choosing the right fabric is the most important step when it comes to learning how to sew because it really can make or break a project. Let me give you an example. Imagine a sofa in front of you. You'll want to be able to sit on it comfortably, so it can't be too hard or too soft. It's the exact same idea when you're making your own clothes. You'll want to choose fabric because of how it looks, but you'll need to make sure it's not so stiff that you can't move freely or so floppy that it doesn't hold the shape you want. Of course, you can play with fabric to create unusual pairings and unique fashion details. But for the most part, in this book, you'll want to choose beginner-friendly fabrics that are easy to handle.

Now you're probably wondering what makes a fabric easy to sew. Generally speaking, you'll want to use a fabric that cuts easily and doesn't slip and slide around much. If it's too slippery or fine, it's going to be really tricky to cut precisely, and it might even get stuck in your machine when sewing!

You'll also want to make sure you're using good-quality fabrics when sewing your final garments. That doesn't necessarily mean you need to use really expensive fabric; it's actually better to practise with cheaper ones first. This is so you can test the pattern and your skills before cutting out your beautiful fabric. Remember that sewing is all about practice, and I can't stress enough that the more you allow yourself to play and have fun, the easier it will be to learn how to handle different types of fabrics. Everything is a learning curve, and it's not a failure if you learnt something! Let me talk you through my favourite beginner-friendly fabrics, starting with woven fabrics, which are the easiest to start off with.

WOVEN FABRICS

Woven fabrics don't tend to stretch unless they are cut on the bias (a more advanced technique) and these fabrics will be easiest to handle if you've never sewn before. There are many different variations but here are three beginner-friendly options.

Cotton is the most popular fabric in the world. It's a natural plant fibre that is soft and fluffy. It's also known as the most beginner-friendly type of fabric because it's stable, lightweight and can be ironed at a high heat. If you've never sewn anything before, start with cotton.

Linen is made from another natural plant fibre called flax. It's a fabric that is durable, easy to handle and perfect for beginners. Compared to cotton, linen can feel stiffer and crisper, but it usually softens after multiple washes. You can iron linen at a high heat, which is definitely needed because it's more prone to wrinkling! Note that it's best to dry linen garments flat as the fairly loose weave makes this fabric prone to stretching.

Rayon, also known as viscose, is classed as a semi-synthetic fibre because although it is made from natural fibres, its production requires chemical processing. Viscose rayon is made from wood pulp, but some forms of rayon contain other fibres including cotton and bamboo. It was created to be an affordable imitation of silk, so as you can imagine it's smooth and soft and has a lustrous appearance. It's a good beginner fabric to try if you want your clothes to have more drape and movement. Be aware that it is prone to wrinkling and needs to dry flat to prevent it from losing its shape.

STRETCH FABRICS

Once you see the stretch patterns in this book, you'll want to work with stretchy fabric. Stretch or knit fabrics are made by combining loops of thread or yarn to create a much more flexible fabric than one that has been woven. It can be super comfortable to wear and allows for weight fluctuations because it will naturally fit your body. Jersey fabrics will be perfect for all the stretch patterns in this book. Note that many stretch fabrics also include elastic materials such as elastane, Lycra or spandex, which help the fabric spring back into shape.

Jersey is a knit fabric that can be made using mixed fibres, pure cotton, wool or synthetics. It's lightweight, smooth and soft, so it's perfect for T-shirts, dresses, underwear and sportswear. Jersey edges tend to curl after cutting, but you can always use a little spray starch to keep the fabric flat while you are sewing. Standard jersey is also called single jersey, but you can also buy double jersey, which is thicker, interlocked jersey, ribbed jersey (see right) and more. They all vary in characteristics, and some will be more drapey, more slinky or sturdier than others.

BUYING SWATCHES

Now, let's say you're browsing online for fabric, and you come across fabric types you've never sewn or felt before. I would always recommend ordering swatches before committing to buy any amount of fabric because you want to make sure it's going to work with the project you have in mind. The number of times I've ordered fabric that looks nice and lightweight online, only to discover once it has come to my door that it's completely see-through, or it's so delicate that my machine can't handle it. And sometimes the colour is different from what I thought when viewing it on a screen. It's hard to truly capture what fabric looks like online, so if you get the chance, pop to a local fabric shop or even look inside your wardrobe to be able to feel the different fabric types and see how they behave.

MORE CHALLENGING FABRICS

If you're a complete beginner, I would stick with the fabrics we've already talked about to start with, but once you feel more confident with your machine and have already sewn several projects you can give the following fabrics a go. I know these fabrics look super pretty, but they can be much trickier to handle, so hold off on these until you're ready for a challenge!

Silk is a natural fibre that is produced from the cocoons of silkworms. We all know silk has a luxurious touch and looks expensive because of its smooth and drapey appearance. It's lightweight, so it needs to be ironed on a low heat, and it is very slippery to work with. Traditional methods of extracting the silk threads from the cocoons involve killing the silkworms, so if you like the idea of wearing silk but want to choose environmentally and ethically better fabrics, look out for peace silk, which is produced more sustainably and without killing the silkworms.

Chiffon can be made with natural or synthetic fibres and is known for its very lightweight and sheer appearance. It flows gracefully to create garments that move beautifully and look perfect for evening wear. It varies in opacity so it can be very sheer and see-through, and this lightness means it is also very slippery and hard to handle.

Ribbed knit is a type of knit fabric that has distinct vertical columns running down the fabric. It is stretchier than single jersey and can hug the body better. It doesn't wrinkle and the edges don't curl once cut. However, ribbed knit can have a tendency to stretch out when you're sewing it, so it's important to stabilize any necklines and armholes to prevent this.

The idea of starting a new project is always so exciting. Being able to bring your vision to life with fabric and a sewing machine is incredible and being able to then love what you made is even better. Try ordering a few samples of the different types of fabric I've mentioned to see how they differ in terms of softness, weight, stretch and opacity. Or, if you are lucky enough to live close to a large fabric shop, take the time to wander around and familiarize yourself with all the different fabric types.

HOW TO MEASURE YOUR BODY TO PICK A SIZE

If you walked into three different fashion shops and bought a small T-shirt at each one, they might not all fit the same. The first might be too tight at the bust, the second might be too loose at the waist and the last might be too long. You can't simply walk into every shop and expect a T-shirt to fit in the exact same way because their size charts vary. The same applies to sewing patterns.

Every pattern designer uses their own size chart so it's super important to measure your body and pick a size based on that. Also, if you're going to the effort of sewing your own clothes, you might as well take the time to measure yourself and make garments that fit you. I like to measure myself every few months to make sure I'm still sewing the right size for my body.

Take a flexible tape measure and follow the illustration on the opposite page to accurately take your measurements. The three main measurements you'll need to take are your full bust, waist and hip sizes. For many of the other measurements it is helpful to enlist the assistance of a friend because it can be difficult to measure yourself properly as you will need to stand up straight but with a relaxed pose for accurate results.

Hints & Tips

If you find any of your bust, waist or hip measurements land between two sizes (e.g. your bust is a size 10 and your waist is a size 12), you have options. Check out the finished garment measurements (see opposite) as this will help you decide which size will give you the fit you want.

- Choose the bigger size: you can always take in the excess fabric where the garment is loose, but you can't add fabric where it is too tight.

- Grade the pattern by taking the cutting line from one size to the next in the appropriate areas to suit your body measurements (see page 26).

1 **Full bust:** Wrap the tape measure around your entire bust, making sure the back is not twisted and is straight. The tape should lie across your nipples as this will be the fullest point. If you wear a bra underneath your clothing, make sure to wear this when you're taking this measurement.

2 **Waist:** Wrap the tape measure around the smallest part of your waist. This is normally a few inches above your belly button.

3 **Hips:** Wrap the tape measure around your hips and bottom. You want it to go around the fullest part of your hips, which will naturally lie across the fullest part of your bottom.

It's also useful to take extra measurements to help alter the pattern to fit as you desire. Some of these are only applicable to certain garments.

4 **Height:** Measure from the top of your head to the floor, with your feet flat on the ground.

5 **Inner leg/inseam:** Measure from the top of your leg on the inner side/crotch down to your ankle.

6 **High bust:** Wrap the tape measure around your high bust, which is above your bust and right under your arms. Make sure the tape measure is not twisted and is straight across your back and that your arms are down, otherwise the measurement won't be accurate.

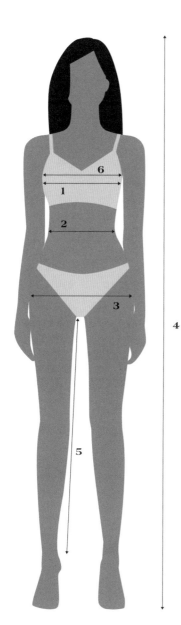

WHAT ARE FINISHED GARMENT MEASUREMENTS?

Put on any top from your wardrobe, and unless it's made from stretchy fabric you should notice it has excess fabric around the bust and waist. Garments will have different amounts of ease, which essentially is just extra room to allow for your body to move freely. Ease will determine how fitted or loose your garment will be after it is sewn, and styles that are designed to be figure-hugging will have less ease than those that are designed to be loose and flowing. If you compare the finished garment measurements to the size chart, you'll notice the numbers in each project will differ.

For patterns designed to be sewn with woven fabrics the finished garment measurements will be larger than the corresponding body measurements because there is positive ease in the garment. Stretch garments sometimes have negative ease, so the finished garment measurements will be smaller than the body measurements – this is because the fabric will stretch over your body for a close fit. It's important to look at both the finished garment measurements and the size chart to determine what size you should sew because you can then pick how tight or loose you want the garment to be. Also, if you're between sizes, the finished garment measurements might show that there is enough ease for you to choose the smaller size.

WHAT ABOUT LENGTH ADJUSTMENTS?

Sometimes it's not the width measurements that cause fitting issues but the length. The patterns in this book have been drafted for someone with a height of 5ft 6in (168cm) and if you are taller or shorter than this you may need to lengthen or shorten the pattern pieces to fit you better. In this case, see Basic Pattern Adjustments on page 27 for information on adjusting pattern lengths.

USING PATTERNS

Before you start working with any sewing patterns in this book, it's helpful to know how to read them. When you first look at a sewing pattern you might feel overwhelmed with what all the markings and symbols mean. They all have their purpose and I'll take you through what they mean to clear up any confusion. This book contains digital sewing patterns, but you can use this guide to help you read any sewing pattern confidently.

CUTTING LINES

On any sewing pattern you look at, you'll notice cutting lines. These are used to help differentiate each size and can be shown in colour or black and white. The patterns in this book use black lines that differ in style with varying dots and dashes to clearly show each size. It can be overwhelming to look at all the lines at once because some may overlap each other. In this case you can select the sizes you want to see before printing to help you easily read the sewing patterns. Once printed you can also use a highlighter and draw over the cutting line for the size you want to sew. This will help you visualise where you need to cut. If at any point you forget what size you're cutting you can find the size key on the pattern and use this to refer to. See opposite for an example of a size key.

NOTCHES

You may also notice small dashes on certain areas of the sewing pattern. These are called notches and can also appear as small triangular shapes at the edges of a pattern piece. They are used to help align pattern pieces correctly and usually appear as single notches. You might find double notches when sewing areas like the sleeves to distinguish the front from the back easily. You can mark notches with chalk or cut into them with scissors, just make sure you cut within the seam allowance so you don't see them in the final garment.

GRAINLINE

When placing your pattern onto fabric you'll want to lie the grainline correctly to make sure the fabric hangs right once sewn. This is the line on the pattern that has a double-headed arrow. The straight grain runs parallel to the selvedge edges of the fabric, so simply align the straight arrow so it runs parallel to the edge. Some patterns get you cut your pattern pieces on the bias, which involves aligning the grainline at a 45 degree angle. This allows the garment to have more stretch and drape once worn but it is a more advanced technique as it's tricker to sew.

LENGTHEN AND SHORTEN LINES

All sewing patterns are drafted for a certain height, in this book they are drafted for someone with a height of 5ft 6in (168cm), so you may need to make adjustments to fit you correctly. On the pattern piece you may notice lengthen and shorten lines, these indicate the correct area to adjust the height of your pattern piece. If the sewing pattern has a fairly simple shape, you can easily lengthen or shorten from the bottom of the garment instead (see page 27).

DARTS

Some sewing patterns will include a dart which looks like a triangular shape, usually starting from one edge towards the centre. The darts in this book follow the same cutting line style as your size to help you easily find the right one. When cutting out your pattern pieces you'll want to keep the dart in tack and not cut into it, but around it. This is so you can use it for reference later. There are many ways you can mark and sew a dart (see page 58) to show you a simple method.

CUT ON FOLD LINES

To help save paper when printing a pattern, some designers choose to only show one half of a symmetrical pattern piece. In this case, you'll find a note instructing you to 'cut on the fold line' on the patterns. You'll need to fold your fabric and align the edge of the pattern piece with the edge of the folded fabric, (see page 35) for how to cut out your fabric. Make sure to refer to the pattern layouts at the start of the pattern instructions before cutting your fabric out.

TRACING

All the patterns in this book are available as digital files you can print them as many times as you like. But if you've got a printed pattern, or you want to retain all the sizes you've printed, I have a handy way to do this. You'll want to get hold of some tracing paper and lay your pattern flat on a table. Before cutting any size out, take a sheet of tracing paper and lay this on top of the pattern. Using a pencil and ruler, carefully copy the pattern pieces onto the tracing paper and remember to include all the markings. You'll also want to take note of the sizes you've traced and mark the name of each pattern piece. Now you'll have an exact replica of the pattern and you can use this to cut your fabric out of, without having to ruin the original.

KEY

Size	Line
6	·· ·· ··· ··· · ·· ··· ·· · ·· ··· ··· ·· ··· ··
8	——————————————
10	– – – – – – – – – –
12	·– ·· ––– ·· ––· ·· ––– ·· –·– ·· –··
14	·································
16	· · · · · · · · · · · · · · · · · ·
18	— · — · — · — · — ·
20	– – – – – – – – – – – – –
22	· — · —· — · —· —· —·
24	— — — — — — —
26	— · — · – · — — · ·
28	— — — — — —
30	— — — —
32	— — — — — —

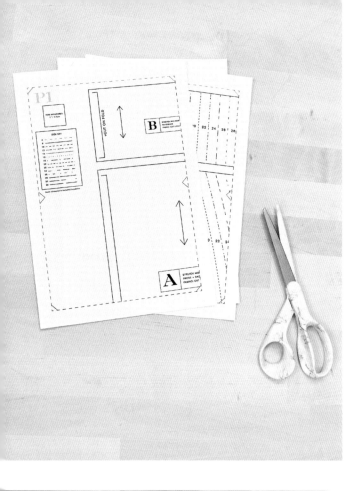

HOW TO PRINT & ASSEMBLE A DIGITAL PATTERN

All the patterns in this book are full-size digital patterns that can be accessed online by scanning the QR code on page 9 to download them. If you've never used a digital pattern before, this section will guide you through every step of the way.

Sewing patterns have traditionally existed in a printed format that you receive physically. However, printed patterns can be more expensive to buy and limit you to having one copy. The number of times I've accidentally cut out the wrong size and then had to buy another copy is eye watering, so over the years I've found I prefer using digital patterns. With a digital pattern you can download it instantly and print as many copies as you want, forever. Which is perfect for me as I'm always losing small pattern pieces!

The digital sewing patterns included in this book come in two different formats. If you want to print your sewing pattern at home using a standard printer, open the 'A4/US letter' file. This document can be printed on both A4 and US letter paper which I'll explain how to do in a moment. If you don't fancy printing the pattern yourself, you can send the 'A0' file to a professional printing shop which will print at a larger scale, meaning you won't need to tape any pages together. If you have a projector, you'll be able to project the A0 patterns and size you need.

To print the pattern on a standard home printer, open the file in any preview software such as Adobe Acrobat by double clicking it. Once it's open you'll notice there will be multiple pages that need to be printed and stuck together. The joy of using digital patterns is that you can either print all the sizes out or you can select just the sizes you want to use – if you're using Adobe Acrobat, open the 'layers' panel and 'hide' or uncheck the layers you don't want to print. This is useful if you find it hard to follow the cutting lines for your size as it will make the pages less cluttered and easier to read. If you are undecided on several sizes, you can print multiple sizes and then grade between them to alter the pattern so it's tailored to your body. See page 26 for more information on how to grade a pattern.

HOW TO PRINT A PATTERN

The most important step when printing a sewing pattern is to make sure your file is set to the correct scale, so it will print at the right size. This can appear on screen as a simple box that needs checking that says 'print 100% to scale' or it may have a scale box where you need to type in '100%'. You can also select a box that reads 'actual size'. Always test print the first page before printing the entire pattern to check you have the correct scale to prevent any paper wastage. The first page of every pattern in this book includes a square box that measures 1 x 1in (2.5 x 2.5cm). Put a ruler against this box to make sure it has printed at the correct scale, then print the rest of your pattern.

HOW TO ASSEMBLE PATTERN PAGES

Each page of the pattern has multiple markings to help you assemble it easily. The last page shows the layout of the printed pattern once assembled. Use this as a guide to show you the order in which the pages need to be attached to each other. There are also page numbers that are marked in the top left hand corner to help you too. There will be a gap around each edge of the pages to allow you to stick or glue them together. The black, rectangular dotted lines mark the edges of the page which you can cut to assemble together. You'll also notice there are six triangular shapes on each page, which need to be aligned to create a diamond shape. All these markings will ensure the pages are correctly attached.

You can either use glue or tape to assemble a digital sewing pattern. Make sure, before you begin, that you have the pages in order, either stacked in order number or laid out in front of you, and then follow this easy method of joining the pages.

Start with the first page in front of you and then cut the left-hand edge of the next page at the dotted rectangular line. Align the cut edge to the right side of the first page to overlap them and tape or glue it to secure it. Repeat until you get to the end of your first row. Once you get to the next row, cut the top edge of the pattern and align it to the bottom of the very first page and tape. Then on the next page, cut the top and left edge and align it to the previous page and tape. Repeat these steps until your full pattern is assembled. There are other methods of joining your pages, but I prefer this method as it will provide a clean and easy-to-read pattern.

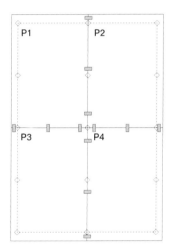

Sewing Tip

Print out just the first page of the pdf pattern first to check that your printer settings are correct and that the square is exactly 1in (2.5cm). Once you're happy with the settings, go ahead and print out the other pages – this stops you wasting printing ink and paper if your settings were wrong the first time.

HOW TO GRADE A PATTERN

Before cutting out your sewing pattern, make sure to look at the size chart for each pattern and compare it to your own body measurements. If you find that, for example, your bust and waist are a size 12 but your hips are a size 14 or 16, you'll need to grade the pattern and alter it to your personal body measurements.

Grading a pattern allows you to combine different sizes easily by drawing new lines to connect the appropriate cutting lines together. Before you start grading from one size to another, it's important to take into account the ease of the garment, which you can find by looking at the garment's finished measurements, as you might find there is sufficient ease included so that grading isn't necessary.

Before printing off your sewing pattern, you'll notice on the digital file that you are able to select multiple sizes. Print only the sizes you fall in between, so it's easier to switch between the sizes you'll be using.

Decide on the sizes that you'll be using at the key areas (bust, waist and hips), then take a pencil and draw a smooth curved line connecting the multiple sizes together at the points you wish to alter. In the previous example, if your bust and waist are a size 12 but your hips are a size 16, draw a line softly transferring from the size 12 cutting line to the size 16 cutting line just below your waist. This will give you a new line to follow and a pattern piece that is graded to your body measurements. Don't forget to repeat the same grading adjustments for all parts of the pattern in those key areas, remembering both the back and front pieces.

An example of grading the hips to be bigger

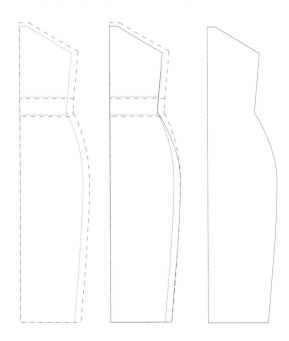

BASIC PATTERN ADJUSTMENTS

To achieve a better fit for your personal measurements you can use these simple pattern adjustments. It's essential to make these changes on your pattern pieces before you cut out your final fabric and it's even better to make a test garment in cheaper fabric to assess the fit. This book shares some simple adjustments you can make to elevate your handmade pieces.

ADJUSTING THE LENGTH

The patterns in this book have been drafted for someone 5ft 6in (168cm) tall, so you might find you need to lengthen or shorten the pattern pieces depending on your height. On a pattern piece you will find a lengthen and shorten line that will be where you will make your adjustment. You can also make this adjustment by simply adding to the hem edge.

HOW TO LENGTHEN A PATTERN

If there's a lengthen/shorten line on the pattern piece you need to adjust, cut across it. Decide how much extra length you want to add, then take a piece of paper and slide it behind the pattern pieces. Fill in the gap with the paper and tape the top section of the pattern piece down onto it. Make marks on the new piece of paper that are the same distance from the top pattern section as the extra length you want to add and join them up with a line. In this example, I am adding 2in (5cm) to the length. Now align the bottom section of the pattern piece with the line and tape it down. Connect the broken lines at the sides of the pattern with a pencil and cut the excess paper away. This is your new pattern piece.

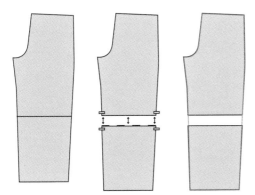

If there is no lengthen/shorten line, first decide how much length you need or want to add. Then take a piece of paper and tape it to the wrong side of the bottom of the pattern piece. Draw a line parallel to the existing hem to add the extra length and then draw another line to extend the pattern piece side seams to match the new line. Cut the excess paper away. This is your new pattern piece.

HOW TO SHORTEN A PATTERN

If there's a lengthen/shorten line on the pattern piece you need to adjust, cut across it. Decide how much length you want to remove, then overlap the top and bottom sections of the pattern by this amount. In this example I am removing 2in (5cm) from the length. Tape the pattern together and smooth any mismatched lines at the sides by redrawing them with a pencil. This is your new pattern piece.

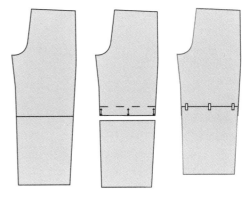

If there is no lengthen/shorten line, decide how much length you need or want to remove. Then draw a line parallel to the existing hem and above it – the distance of the new line from the existing hem should be equal to the amount of length you wish to remove. Cut the excess pattern away. This is your new pattern piece.

FULL-BUST ADJUSTMENT

Like many commercial patterns, the designs in this book have been drafted for a B cup size. This means that the difference between the high-bust and full-bust measurements (see page 20) is 2in (5cm). If you find that clothes that fit across your bust tend to be baggy above the bust and that tops are often shorter at the front than the back, chances are that you are a D cup or above and you need to do a full-bust adjustment. The resulting garment will fit better and be more flattering, and once you've done the adjustment the first time, it will be much easier to do it on other patterns too.

To do a full-bust adjustment, you won't be working with the pattern piece that fits your full-bust measurement but the one that matches your high-bust measurement. To find this size, measure your high bust (see page 20) and add 2in (5cm). Now look at the size chart for the pattern you are making and find the size which has a bust size that is the amount you calculated (your high bust plus 2in/5cm) or slightly larger. This is the pattern size you will be working with.

You also need to note down how much larger your bust is than the bust size in the chart for the size you will be working with. For example, if your high bust is 37in (94cm) then you want to use the pattern size for a bust of 39in (99cm), and if your bust is actually 40in (101.5cm), then you need to increase the bust area by 1in (2.5cm).

Divide this measurement in half as you will be working on one half of the bodice front. In this example, the increase required will be ½in (1.2cm). Don't worry – that's all the maths done with!

You'll need plenty of paper for this process, so either tape some A4/US letter paper together or, ideally, use a large roll of paper, flattened out brown paper from packaging or large sheets of tracing paper.

WOVEN BODICE WITH SIDE DARTS

Making a full-bust adjustment to a bodice with darts in woven fabric is easiest if the bust darts run to the side seams as on the Camisole and the Button-back Top, so these are good pattern choices for your first full-bust adjustment.

1. First, trace the front bodice pattern in the appropriate size, including the lines of the front dart. You only want to work on one half of the front bodice, which for the Camisole is the pattern as provided but for the Button-back Top you will need to fold the pattern in half vertically and then trace off the half pattern. Next, hold the pattern up to your body and mark where your nipple is – this is called the bust point.

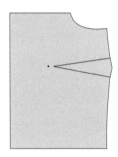

2. Now draw three lines on the pattern – I recommend using a different coloured pen for these to help you distinguish them from the lines of the existing dart. Draw the first line (A) parallel to the centre front (where you will cut the pattern on the fold), from the bottom edge of the bodice to the bust point. Next, draw a line from the bust point to the armhole, anywhere along the bottom third of the armhole (B) – it doesn't matter exactly where. Mark a dot on this line that is about ³⁄₈in (1cm) from the armhole edge. Finally, draw a line from the bust point to the outer angle of the dart, where the centre fold line of the dart is (C).

3. Cut up from the lower edge of the bodice to the bust point along line (A), then cut along line (B) until you reach the dot. If you accidentally cut all the way to the armhole, tape that last ³⁄₈in (1cm) back together as we need this hinge of paper. Finally, cut along line (B) from the outer edge at the side seam nearly up to the dart point – as before you need to leave a small hinge of paper uncut.

4. Pull the pattern apart at line (A) by the amount you calculated that you need to add to the bust – half the difference between the pattern's bust size and yours. The centre of the bodice will stay put while the side will move out and down. Slip some paper behind the pattern, double check that the gap at line (A) is the correct width and then stick everything down. Allow extra paper to extend beyond the dart on the side seam.

5. The bottom of the pattern no longer matches up. To fix this, cut a horizontal line across from the centre front to join the cut at line (A). Lower the section below the cut until it is in line with the lowest part of your pattern. Again, fill the gap in the pattern with paper applied from underneath and stick it in place.

2.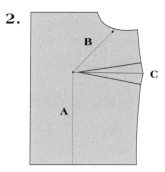

3.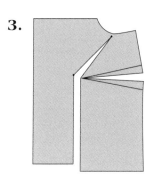

5.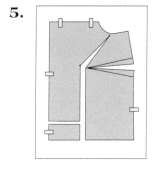

6. 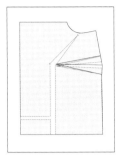 **7.**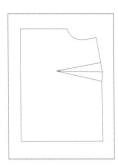

6. Measure between the top and bottom lines of the dart (which is now wider than it was) at the side-seam edge and mark a dot in the middle on this edge. Draw a line running from this point to your bust point. Measure 1½in (4cm) out along this line, starting at the bust point, and make a dot. This is going to be the inner end of the new dart as, on a fuller bust, a dart that doesn't go all the way to the nipple looks much better. Draw your new dart from this point to the top and bottom of the dart on the side-seam edge. Fold up your new dart as if you have stitched and pressed it, and cut along the side-seam edge, cutting through the folded paper as one. Trim off any other extra paper.

7. The waistline will now be wider than in the original pattern but remember that you started with a pattern smaller than your bust size so this may be fine. Check with the sizes in the charts, and if you need to, take in the side seam at the waist to fit you, taking a quarter of the excess amount from the front and back side-seam edges. (You only need to reduce by a quarter of the full amount because the reductions are repeated on both sides of the garment.)

STRETCH BODICE WITHOUT DARTS

Stretch fabric is wonderful because it's not only comfortable, but it's also very accommodating. This means that you don't usually need to make a full-bust adjustment, especially if you choose a fabric that has a lot of stretch, such as Lycra. Make sure that if the fabric stretches more in one direction than the other, you cut out the pattern with the greatest stretch giving ease to the width, not the length. If you do still need to do a full-bust adjustment, the process is essentially the same as for a woven bodice with side darts with a few adaptations.

1. Start by following step 1 on page 28. Draw on the three lines as in step 2 – there is no dart, so just draw line (C) out to the side-seam edge. This could be a horizontal line, but if the bust point is higher than the bottom of the armhole, draw this as a line sloping down to the side seam.

2. Continue on, following steps 3–5 for the woven bodice adjustment. You now have a gap in the side seam which is basically a dart. To get rid of it, draw a line from the top of the side-seam gap to the bust point and from the bottom of the gap to the bust point. Cut out this triangle of paper. Now draw a line parallel to the centre front from the bottom of the bodice to the bust point. Cut along this line almost to the bust point, leaving a small hinge of paper. Close up the triangle you cut from the side seam and stick the edges together. The side seam will swing out to the side and the vertical cut will open out.

3. Slip some paper behind the triangular gap in the pattern below the bust point and stick it in place. Draw a line connecting the two bottom sections of the bodice together. This is your cutting line for the hem. Notice that the lower edge is now wider, which is probably fine for a tank top or T-shirt but not ideal in a close-fitting garment such as the Halter-neck Dress, which is why opting for a super-stretchy fabric instead of doing a full-bust adjustment is often the best solution.

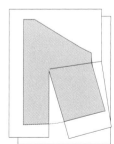 

SMALL-BUST ADJUSTMENT

If, instead of needing to make the bust larger you need to make it smaller, simply follow the steps on pages 28–30 for a woven bodice but instead of spreading the pattern by half the amount you wish to add in step 4, overlap it by half the amount you need to remove. In step 5 you will then need to raise the centre part of the pattern instead of lowering it.

HAVE YOU SEWN SOMETHING & YOU NOW HATE IT?

It can be beyond frustrating to spend hours sewing a garment, only to realize at the end that you hate it and it doesn't live up to your expectations. It happens to all of us and it's hard not to let that bring you down or make you want to give up on sewing entirely! I've got a handful of tips to help you figure out what to do about it!

1 IT JUST LOOKS BAD...

Sewing is a skill that ultimately gets better with practice, but also with patience. If, when you put on the garment, you notice that nothing really lays as it should or the seams look puffy and misshapen, this might be because you didn't iron your seams! Ironing might sound incredibly boring but taking the time to iron every seam after you've sewn it will really help the garment sit correctly and look super professional. A small step like not rushing your project by sewing at a slower pace instead of pushing it through the machine will also make the final garment look and fit so much better. So don't give up but go slower next time.

2 IT'S NOT REALLY MY STYLE...

When I first started sewing, I just assumed that I had to make everything in a cotton fabric because that's what everyone else was making. I didn't realize that only a few pieces in my own wardrobe were actually made out of cotton and it's a fabric that I only wore on a few occasions. It's such a helpful step in the process of making your own clothes to look in your personal wardrobe and assess the garments you love to wear on repeat. What do they look like? What fabric(s) are they made of? Are they in a printed fabric or a plain colour? Do you like to wear fitted or looser clothes? All of these questions will help you narrow down what you like to wear and emulate those styles when sewing.

3 IT DOESN'T FEEL COMFORTABLE...

There are many reasons why the garment you've sewn might feel uncomfortable or restricting. The most common reason is because you've sewn a size too small, so the garment might be digging in at certain areas or it's so small that there isn't any ease to help you move. I recommend you retake your measurements with a flexible measuring tape and if you can, get someone else to do this so your body is relaxed. There are other factors that can impact how comfortable a garment feels, such as whether you've chosen a fabric that's too stiff and rigid so that it doesn't naturally drape over your body. Or in your personal wardrobe you might realize you normally wear elastic-waisted bottoms, so if you sew tailored trousers/pants it might be a different style of garment than you're used to. Ultimately, you'll need to practise and experiment with different fabrics, patterns and styles to find the type of garment you love to sew and wear!

4 QUICK FIXES TO TRY

Don't let a garment you don't like gather dust, there are a few simple hacks you can try to spruce it up. The easiest one is to chop off the hem and make it shorter. You'll be surprised at how different a dress can look at different lengths, so if you made a midi or a maxi length, try cutting it into a mini! If you find the overall garment really isn't doing anything for your style, then try to salvage any bigger bits of fabric from areas like the skirt to upcycle into a crop top, tote bag, scrunchies or smaller projects.

C

SCRUNCHIE
FABRIC: CUT 1 ON THE FOLD

HOW TO CUT YOUR FABRIC

Now comes the scariest bit of all – cutting into your fabric! If you're a complete beginner, you'll want to practise on cheaper fabric before splurging on the expensive stuff. Before you take your scissors out and start cutting, you need to prewash your fabric. Many of us are guilty of skipping this crucial step but prewashing your fabric will make sure your garment, once sewn, won't shrink or distort in the wash. All you need to do is put the entire fabric piece in your washing machine and wash and then dry it as you normally would, then once it's completely dry give it a press with your iron to smooth any wrinkles. If you cut your pattern out of wrinkled fabric it can distort the final garment which may mean that it won't hang correctly once worn.

Next, if you haven't already done so, select the pattern you want to sew and take a look at the pattern layout so you can see the recommendation of how to lay the patterns onto your fabric. Generally, you'll want to fold the fabric in half with right sides together and align the selvedges/selvages together. Make sure the folded edge is parallel to the selvedges. Smooth the fabric out so there are no wrinkles and so that the folded edge is flat and not twisted.

If your pattern piece is cut on the fold, you'll need to align the edge of the pattern piece, where the cut-on-fold lines are, to the edge of the folded fabric. This will mean it will be doubled when we open it out after cutting. Make sure the grainlines on all pattern pieces are facing the correct way and are parallel to the fabric selvedges/selvages.

You can either use pins to hold the pattern down on the fabric or you can use pattern weights. I like to use metal washers or even food cans to keep my pattern pieces in place, but be wary if the object is too heavy as it can distort the fabric. Once your patterns are secured to your fabric, use scissors or a rotary cutter and cutting mat to cut your pattern pieces out. Remember to cut any notches and mark any darts, and if your fabric wrong side looks very similar to the right side, it might be worth using some chalk to mark your pattern pieces on the wrong sides.

Take your time when cutting your pattern pieces, especially if you're dealing with slippery fabrics. I find it easier to cut long strides with scissors rather than smaller cuts for an even edge. If you're cutting around a curved edge, then smaller cuts may make it easier to follow precisely. A pair of good dressmaking scissors will make all the difference when cutting your fabric, so be sure to invest in a good pair!

CORE SEWING TECHNIQUES

Here you'll find a set of sewing
techniques that will not only help
you to sew the patterns in this book
but will empower you to tackle other
sewing projects and even make a
few adaptations to the patterns to suit
your own style and requirements.

HOW TO SEW A SEAM

Sewing a seam is the easiest skill to master and you'll be able to pick this up in no time! A seam is where two pieces of material are attached together by a stitching line. There are a few key steps to follow to make sure your seams look nice and smooth.

SEWING WOVEN FABRICS

The most basic seam involves sewing two pieces of woven fabric together with a straight stitch. For this exercise, you'll want to take two small pieces of fabric that are the same size (4 x 4in/10 x 10cm) and align the two pieces along one edge. Make sure both right sides are together – this is when the pretty sides of the fabric are facing each other.

1. Use pins or clips to hold the fabric edges together temporarily, making sure that the edges are aligned. Line up the top edge of the fabric with the edge of the sewing-machine foot/presser foot, then lower the foot so you can start sewing. (Depending on the width of your sewing foot and the seam allowance required, you may need to adjust the positioning of your fabric when sewing a garment, but for this exercise, you can use the width of the sewing foot as your guide.)

2. Start by sewing forwards a few stitches and then stitch backwards a few stitches to prevent the seam from unravelling. Slowly continue sewing down the seam, removing the pins as you go and then backstitch at the end. Backstitching at the beginning and end is super important because it's similar to tying a knot that holds the stitches in place. Remember to take your time when sewing a seam – there's no rush to get it done as quickly as possible and it will allow you to construct a garment neatly.

3. Once you've finished sewing your seam, raise the sewing foot, pull the fabric out from under it and cut the excess bobbin and needle thread. If you're using an advanced machine there may be an automatic thread-cutter button that cuts the thread for you.

4. Ta-da! You've sewn a seam! I like to press my seams with an iron for a neat finish that looks smooth from the right side. There are so many different seam techniques to try but for this book you'll only need to learn this one.

SEWING KNIT FABRICS

When using knit fabrics, you need to use a stitch that will stretch with the material, otherwise your stitching is likely to snap. If you have an overlocker, you can use that to stitch most seams on knitted fabrics, and because it neatens the seam allowances at the same time, it makes quick work of making up your knit garments. If you don't have an overlocker, you can use the stretch stitch on your sewing machine, if it has one, or simply use a narrow zigzag stitch. Once you've set the sewing machine to the chosen stitch, you can stitch your seams in the same way as woven fabrics (see left). Use the same zigzag stitch for hems or try a twin needle (see below) for a professional look.

HOW TO HEM A GARMENT

Double-fold hem: I like to use double hems on my garments because they're neat and easy to sew. For a double hem, fold the fabric over to the wrong side by the amount specified in the pattern and press. Fold the fabric again to enclose the raw edge. This second fold may be the same depth as the first fold or it may be deeper as some garments hang better if they have a deeper hem. Press once more, pin and then stitch close to the fold to complete the hem. You can use this method on both woven and knit fabrics.

Single-fold hem: Some projects require single hems, for example along the sides of the slits in the skirts. For these, all you need to do is finish the seam (see page 38), fold the fabric once by the specified amount, press it and then stitch close to the fold.

Twin-needle hem: A twin needle has two needles on one shank. You thread each needle with a separate top thread, and from the right side of the fabric you will see two parallel rows of stitching, while underneath, the bobbin thread zigzags between the two top threads. The construction of the stitch gives it extra stretch, making it a useful stitch for knit fabrics. When hemming your knits, you can use the same zigzag stitch as you used for your seams, but using a twin needle gives a professional finish.

HOW TO FINISH A SEAM

Once you've sewn a seam, it's important to press the seams and finish the raw edges to neaten them and prevent fraying. Not only will this prolong the durability of the garment, but it also makes the inside of the garment look much better. Depending on the type of fabric you're using, it may fray when you cut and sew the pieces of your pattern or it may fray in the washing machine once you've finished – or both. Fabrics such as cotton fray less than linen, and knit fabrics don't fray at all!

As you continue your sewing journey, you'll come across more seam finishes than the ones I'm going to explain here, but for the purposes of this book I'm keeping things simple. Try testing out these common seam-finish techniques on different fabrics to see how they behave.

OVERLOCKER/SERGER

This method is my preferred way of finishing seams because of the neat result it provides. You will need an overlocker/serger machine which is different from a sewing machine and creates a stitch that combines three or four threads – as a general rule, use four threads to finish seams on medium-weight or heavyweight fabrics and three threads on lightweight fabrics. Align the raw edge of the fabric with the edge of the sewing/presser foot and slowly overlock the edge. As you press down on the overlocker pedal, the fabric edge will be trimmed and two of the threads will pass over the edge to create a neat finish. Be careful when using an overlocker as there is a sharp blade close to the presser foot that trims the excess fabric. Also make sure that there aren't any pins near the fabric edge as the blade can snap or chip if it comes in contact with one.

ZIGZAG STITCH

If you don't have an overlocker, using a zigzag stitch on your sewing machine will be an easy way to finish your seams. Once your seam has been sewn, align the fabric edge with the edge of the presser foot and sew along the raw edge using a zigzag stitch. I like to use a medium length and width (2–2.5mm long and 3–3.5mm wide). If you find the fabric is too lightweight and keeps getting stuck in the machine when sewing, try stitching further away from the edge and then trim the seam afterwards so it's close to the edge of the stitching line.

PINKING SHEARS

The easiest and simplest way to finish a seam is to use pinking shears. Once your seam has been sewn, take your pinking shears and trim the raw edges of the seam allowance. These types of scissors have a serrated edge and the finished edge will look like a line of triangles. Note that this seam finish isn't the most durable and if your fabric frays a lot, it might still fray in the wash.

FRENCH SEAMS

If you're looking for a pretty and durable way to finish a seam, try using a French seam. This finish encloses the seam and is perfect for lightweight fabrics that don't combine well with overlocking/serging or zigzag stitch. Note that if you wish to sew French seams on any of the garments in this book, you will need to increase the size of the seam allowance when cutting out your pieces by an additional ⅜in (1cm).

1. Place both fabric pieces together with wrong sides facing and pin the seam. Sew using a straight stitch and a ⅜in (1cm) seam allowance.

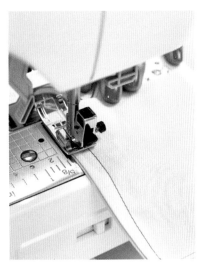

2. Trim the seam allowances in half and press them both flat to one side – if using thicker fabric, grade the seam allowances by trimming one seam allowance a little shorter than the other.

3. Fold the fabric again but this time with the right sides together, making sure the seam lies along the fold.

4. Pin the seam and sew using a straight stitch and a ⅜in (1cm) seam allowance.

5. Press the seam again and you will see that the raw edges have been completely enclosed.

COMMON SEWING PROBLEMS

Sewing can be a fun and enjoyable craft but it does come with its own challenges. It's incredibly frustrating when your seams don't look right or your machine isn't sewing as it should. Here are some common sewing problems and handy tips to help you fix them.

THREAD BUNCHING UP

If you've started sewing a seam and noticed that on the reverse side the thread looks all knotted and tangled (like a bird's nest) then your thread is bunching up. This is easily fixed by rethreading your machine and your bobbin. You also might want to look under your bobbin for any lint or loose thread build-up and brush it away.

SKIPPED STITCHES

This problem can happen on woven and knit fabrics, and it's when your stitches aren't even with some that look extra long. I've always found it's because I'm either using the wrong needle for my fabric type or the needle is dull and not sharp anymore, in which case it needs replacing asap! In fact, it's often recommended that you change the needle after every 6–8 hours of sewing to keep your stitching at its best.

THREAD BREAKING

You know how you see those thread packets that come with 50 colours for £1? Well, they're probably not the best quality! You want to choose high-quality thread to prevent it from snapping or breaking as you're sewing. It's even better if you can match your thread composition with your fabric composition, so if you're sewing with cotton fabric try using cotton thread, and if you're using a mixed-fibre fabric opt for poly-cotton thread, for example. You'll also want to rethread your machine to make sure it's not getting caught on anything sharp or snapping because you simply haven't threaded it correctly.

UNEVEN SEAMS

If the seams of your garment look puffy or uneven, it might be because you haven't pressed them correctly with your iron. You want to make sure that after sewing every seam you take the time to press it, so it has a smooth and crisp appearance. This really does make a difference, because when you join sections of a garment that have nicely pressed seams, your new seam will be smoother. You'll also want to make sure when sewing your seams that you're not rushing the fabric through but working at a slow pace – and make sure you're sewing evenly and at the correct seam allowance too.

WAVY SEAMS ON KNITS

Sewing with knit fabrics can be tricky as a beginner and you might find your seams look wavy once sewn. This can be because the fabric has stretched out whilst you've been sewing. Make sure you're using a zigzag stitch or your machine's stretch stitch and try adjusting the length and width to see what works best for your fabric. If your machine allows you to reduce the presser-foot pressure, this could also reduce any stretching out. You can also use steam and a tailor's clapper (see page 13) to press your seams gently after being sewn to help with any waviness. I always like to test my stitches on scrap pieces of the fabric I'm going to be using, to make sure the seams will look nice.

HOW TO SEW ON BUTTONS

Knowing how to sew on a button is such a handy skill that once you master it, everyone will be asking you to fix theirs! This tutorial is very straightforward and will allow you to stop buttons from falling off easily. You'll want to use thread that matches your fabric and choose suitable buttons – some patterns will specify a size to use, so make sure to choose appropriately.

1. Thread a hand-sewing needle so there's an equal length of thread from both sides. Secure both ends together by tying a knot.

2. Position the button on your fabric: if you made a mark where you want it to sit, align the button to the centre of that mark. If you've already sewn your buttonholes, double check that the button aligns and will slide into the buttonhole smoothly.

3. From the back/wrong side of the fabric, push the needle through the fabric and one hole of your button then pull the thread taut.

4. Go back through another hole in the button and then through your fabric. Keep repeating this process of alternating from sewing from the back to the front until you have sewn enough times for the button to be securely attached. I like to sew at least eight loops. Make sure you don't pull the thread too tight as you need to allow for the thickness of the buttonhole.

5. Finish your last stitch with the needle and thread at the front of your fabric, and instead of taking the needle up through the button, we're going to wrap the thread around the gap between the button and fabric several times in a circular motion. This will create a button shank.

6. Once sewn, tie two knots underneath the button and cut the excess thread away.

STITCHING OPTIONS

Standard buttons have two or four holes. If yours have two holes, you simply bring the needle up through one and go down through the other. If your buttons have four holes you have choices. The standard option is to sew in a cross, going up through one hole and down through the diagonally opposite one. Then bring the needle up through one of the two remaining free holes and go down through the last hole. Repeat the sequence until the button is securely attached. You can also stitch on four-hole buttons by treating each pair of holes separately to create two parallel lines of thread or you can stitch around in a circle, so you have four little stitches.

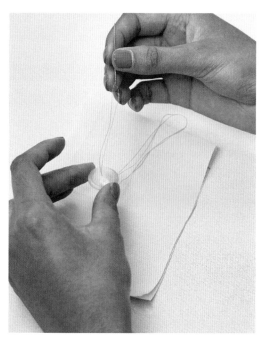

Sewing Tip

Some buttons, such as military buttons and many other metal and novelty buttons, don't have holes in the top. These are called shank(ed) buttons, and they have a little loop underneath – the shank – that you simply stitch through to attach them. Not only do they have a more luxurious look, but you may find them easier to attach.

HOW TO ADD POCKETS TO
ANY PATTERN IN THIS BOOK

Pockets are super convenient to carry essentials without having to bring
a purse or bag, so on this page you'll learn how to add pockets to anything!
Inseam pockets are hidden in the seam of a garment and are very beginner
friendly to sew. You generally sew inseam pockets at the side seam of
a skirt, trousers/pants or a dress and they're perfect if you want a clean,
hidden look. You can trace the pocket template on the next page and use
this in any garment. In this tutorial, I'll be demonstrating this method on
one side seam: you'll probably want to repeat the exact same steps to the
other side seam of the garment you're sewing.

1. Whatever garment you're sewing, finish the raw
edge of the side seam first. This can be done using
an overlocker/serger, zigzag stitch or pinking shears
to ensure a neat finish.

2. Cut out two pocket template/bags and finish the
raw edges.

3. With right sides together, align one pocket bag with
the side seam of the front piece, positioning the
top of the pocket bag 1½in (4cm) below the top
edge of a skirt, for example. Pin and sew using a
⅜in (1cm) seam allowance. Repeat this step on the
corresponding side seam of the back piece to add
the second pocket piece.

4. Fold the pocket bag away from the garment front
piece and press flat. Stitch the pocket close to the
edge of the fold/seam, working through the pocket
piece and the seam allowances, a technique known
as understitching. Repeat on the garment back piece
and press both pieces.

5. With right sides together, place the front main piece
– in this case, the skirt front – on top of the back
main piece, matching the two pocket pieces right
sides together as well, and pin around the pocket
bags and along the side seam. Starting at the top
of the seam, sew the seam with a ⅜in (1cm) seam
allowance. When you reach the seam line of the
pocket, pivot the needle so you can stitch right
around the pocket bag pieces until you get back
to the garment sections. Then pivot again and
carry on stitching down the rest of the seam.

6. Turn the piece to the right side and push the pockets
inside. Press the side seam flat and push the pocket
towards the centre front of your garment. Your
pockets are now neatly enclosed in the side seam.

This is such a simple method that you can use to
add pockets to literally anything! Having said that,
inseam pockets are much easier to sew when using
woven fabric. If you're adding inseam pockets to knit
fabric, I recommend interfacing the side seam to help
prevent the fabric from stretching out. I love adding
pockets to skirts or dresses, so try adding them to
any patterns in this book.

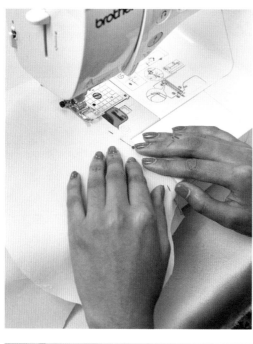

POCKET TEMPLATE

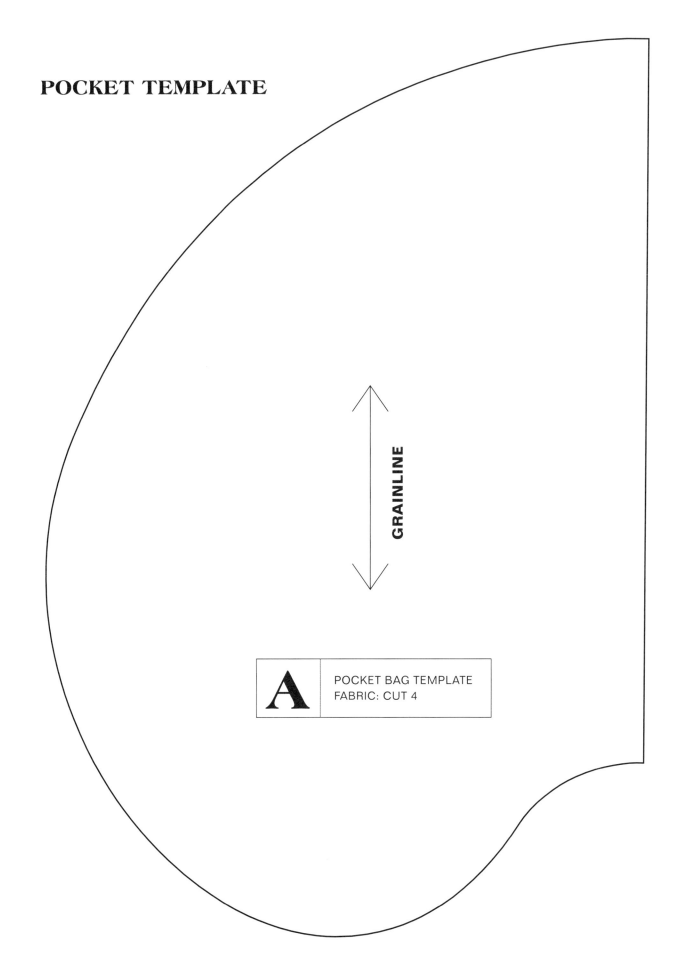

GRAINLINE

A | POCKET BAG TEMPLATE
FABRIC: CUT 4

HOW TO SHIRR FABRIC

Shirring is a wonderful sewing technique for woven fabrics. It involves sewing in rows, using elastic thread in the bobbin and standard thread in the needle, and it gathers the fabric to create a gorgeous texture. Shirred fabric is very comfortable to wear and gives garments a stretchy and adjustable fit, and it's also very much on-trend. In this book you'll find a pattern for a shirred dress and top that make the perfect summer outfits. Here, I'll walk you through the shirring technique step-by-step. Note that it can take a while to find the best settings for your sewing machine, so be prepared to experiment, and once you've found the perfect settings, write them down so you can use them again.

1. Choose a suitable fabric. I recommend a lightweight fabric such as cotton, viscose or poplin as these gather nicely. Gingham fabric is always a good choice because it's lightweight and has a gridded pattern that you can use as a stitching guide.

2. Use a water-soluble pen or chalk to mark the rows of shirring onto your fabric (or follow a stripe if using gingham). You'll want to leave a ½in (1.2cm) or ⅜in (1cm) gap between each row of shirring.

3. Now take your shirring elastic and wind your bobbin by hand, giving it some tension as you wind so it doesn't fall out, but not stretching it tight. Once you've wound your bobbin, insert it into your sewing machine and make sure the elastic thread is pushed into the thread groove of your bobbin.

4. Bring your elastic thread up by turning the hand wheel as you would normally to bring the bobbin thread up and push the thread to the back of the machine. (Even if you're using an automatic machine that would usually do this for you, I recommend doing this step manually with the hand wheel.) Make sure you're only using elastic thread in your bobbin, the top thread will be your standard thread.

5. Shirring settings will vary depending on the machine and the fabric you are using, but I like to set my stitch length to 3–4 and my tension to 6–7. It's important to test shirring on a scrap piece of fabric and play with your settings until you're happy with the stitching, and you will need to stitch at least two lines of stitching before you can really tell if the settings are correct.

6. Place your fabric underneath your presser foot with the right side facing up and begin sewing across one of the rows you marked. As you sew, the elastic thread in the bobbin will start to gather the fabric. Once you get to the end of a row, pivot the fabric and sew down until the next row and pivot once more to start sewing the new row. You'll want to keep sewing in this way until you finish your shirring or your bobbin has run out. If your bobbin does run out, simply backstitch at that point and rewind the bobbin to continue shirring.

7. Once you've sewn a few rows, the shirring detail should be in full effect and if you pull the fabric, it should stretch easily. If you pull the fabric and you feel tension or the elastic thread snaps, you'll need to adjust the settings on your sewing machine until it stretches with no issues.

8. To finish and make the effect even more textured, press the right side of the fabric with your iron and use lots of steam to help it shrink even further.

Sewing Tip

If your elastic looks wobbly once sewn, you need to increase the tension on your bobbin. I recommend rewinding your bobbin with more tension by hand or if your bobbin case has a screw on it, turn this a few times to tighten the bobbin tension. If you do turn that screw, make sure you can remember how to set it back to how it was when you want to go back to regular sewing.

HOW TO GATHER FABRIC

Gathering is a great method for adding fullness to sections of a garment by pulling up one piece of fabric to fit a smaller piece. It's used for the Shirred Dress (see page 86) and is often used on full skirts and full sleeve heads. We will gather the fabric by working a 'gathering stitch'.

You can use the same basic technique to help ease one curved piece to fit another, not to create gathers but to take in a little fullness. I use this technique to help ease fitted sleeves into place, for example on the Tie-front Top and Button-front Dress.

1. Change your machine settings to a longer stitch length such as 4–5 and leave long thread tails at the start. I like to pull at least 4in (10cm) so it's easier to handle as you'll need to hold on to these ends later.

2. Sew a line of stitching just under ⅜in (1cm) from the top edge. This time, once you get to the end don't backstitch but instead pull another 4in (10cm) of thread and cut off at the end. You can also sew another line of stitching in the same way ⅜in (1cm) below the first line if you want more control of how the gathering will sit once sewn.

3. Gently pull the bobbin thread tail to gather the fabric. You'll need to use your fingers to push the fabric towards the middle and then adjust the gathering until it looks even. Make sure the gathered fabric fits the piece you want to attach it to and then recheck the spacing of the gathers: you can tighten or loosen areas by pushing the fabric around.

4. With right sides together, sew the gathered piece to the other piece of fabric, stitching just to the inside of the gathering stitches so you don't see them in the finished garment. Afterwards, you can easily unpick any gathering stitches that show with a seam ripper. I always like to finish the raw edge of this seam using an overlocker/serger but you can use a zigzag stitch on your sewing machine instead. Cut away any loose threads and press your gathered seam for a crisp, neat finish.

Sewing Tip

You can add a gathered detail to any garment – a frill to the bottom of a sleeve or dress, for example. To do this, you simply need to measure the width/circumference of the piece you want to attach it to and multiply that measurement by 1.5–2. This will give you the required length of the new piece you'll need to cut out, which once gathered will fit the original piece. Of course, you also need to decide on the depth of the frill, remembering to add seam/hem allowances.

HOW TO ATTACH KNIT BINDING/BANDS

For the Tank Top pattern, you'll need to add narrow bands of stretch fabric to the neckline and armhole edges. It's a simple and professional way to finish these areas and provides a comfy, neat result. I know that sewing with stretchy fabrics can feel intimidating but with this step-by-step tutorial you'll be sewing with them easily in no time! I am demonstrating the technique with the neck band, but you can follow the same instructions to attach the arm bands, although you can omit the notches at the quarter points.

I normally use an overlocker/serger for these steps, but you can use a stretch stitch or zigzag stitch on your sewing machine in the same way.

1. With right sides together, fold the neck band in half. Align the short ends and sew with a ⅜in (1cm) seam allowance.

2. Once sewn, open out the neck band and fold it in half with wrong sides together. Press the folded edge flat. It'll look like a ring, with the top edge neatly folded and the bottom edges raw.

3. Mark or cut a notch on the opposite side from the centre-back seam and two more notches at the other two quarters of the neckband, keeping the notches within the seam allowance.

4. Mark or cut a notch at the centre front of the neck and centre back of the neck on the bodice as well.

5. Lay out the bodice, right side up. Align the centre-back seam of the neck band to the centre notch on the back bodice piece, making sure that right sides and raw edges are together. Then align the opposite neck band notch with the centre notch of the front bodice piece. Match the two remaining notches to the shoulder seams at the neck. Evenly distribute and pin the rest of the neck band to the neck, making sure it is not twisted. You'll notice the neck band is shorter than the neck opening.

6. Starting from the centre-back seam, sew the neck band to the neckline with a ⅜in (1cm) seam allowance. Because the neck band is smaller than the neck opening, you'll need to stretch the neck band with your fingers as you sew to fit it. I like to work in quarters, so I'll stop and start at the notches as I reposition and stretch the fabric to fit.

7. Once sewn, flip the seam allowance down inside the garment and press the neck band up. You'll want to use a low heat setting on your iron and a pressing cloth to protect the fabric. Make sure there's no puckering and the seam is lying flat.

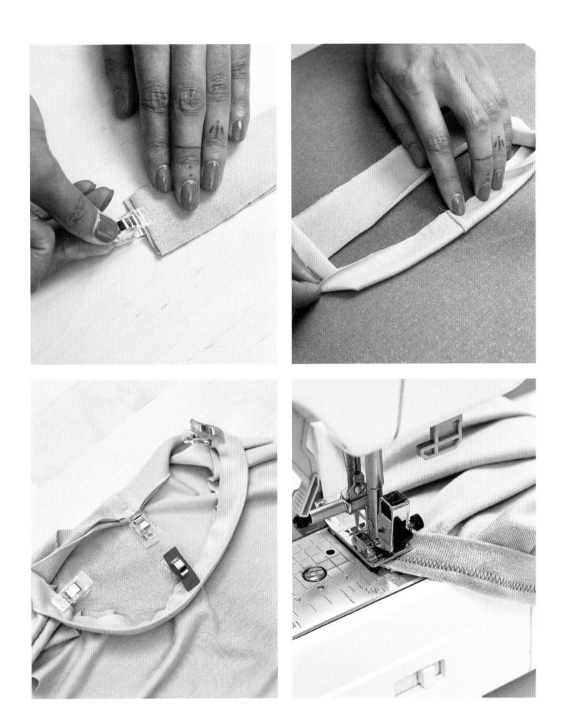

Style Tip

You don't have to use the same fabric for the neck and armhole binding as for the main part of the garment, although it still needs to be a knit fabric. You can even play with contrast binding that is a different colour for a pop of personality!

HOW TO SEW SKINNY STRAPS

Sewing skinny (shoestring/spaghetti) straps can be very fiddly depending on what fabric you're using. I'm going to share two methods you can use, so feel free to use whichever one you find easier! These straps are used for both the Halter-neck Dress (page 112) and Camisole (page 96) patterns of this book. You can use either method on woven or knit fabric, although when sewing with knits I tend to use method 1 which is photographed across.

METHOD 1

1. With right sides together, fold your strap in half and pin the long edges together.

2. Sew along the length with a ⅜in (1cm) seam allowance. Use a straight stitch with woven fabric and a zigzag stitch or overlocker/serger with knit fabrics. You can always increase your seam allowance for an even smaller strap width.

3. Use a loop turner, turning set or safety pin to turn the strap right side out.

4. Press the strap flat for a crisp finish.

METHOD 2

1. Lay out the strap piece, wrong side up. Fold the top long edge over to the wrong side by ⅜in (1cm) and press along the length.

2. Fold the long bottom edge to the wrong side by ⅜in (1cm) and press along the length.

3. Now fold the entire strap in half and press again, making sure the width of the strap is even.

4. Sew along the edge of the strap, through all layers, neatly enclosing the raw edges.

5. Press the strap for a crisp finish.

METHOD 1

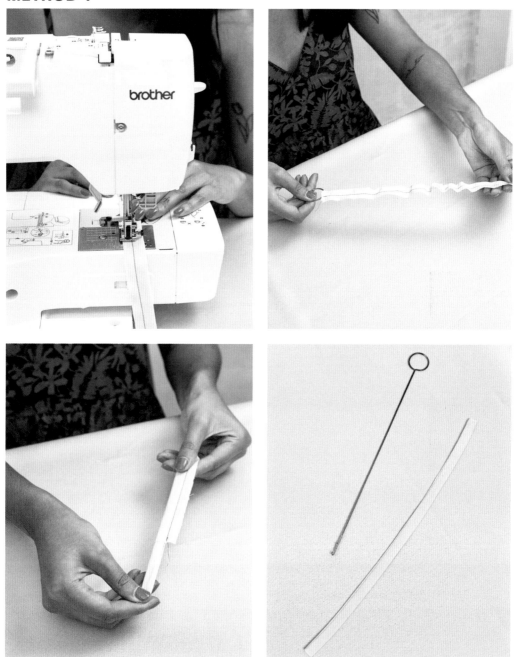

Sewing Tip

If you're working with very light or very heavy fabric, method 1 will be easier to use as you won't need to turn the strap to the right side. Very lightweight fabric can be prone to tearing when you turn narrow straps out and very heavyweight fabric will be too stiff to turn, so it's useful to know both of these methods!

HOW TO SEW A DART

Darts are made by folding your fabric where marked to bring the two long edges of a triangle together and then stitching to create a three-dimensional shape. They are used to create shape in a garment and are commonly sewn at the bust, but you can find them in fitted skirts, trousers/pants and more. They can look tricky to get your head around but once you've tried a few, you'll be able to sew them with ease. You'll find darts in several patterns in this book, so if you haven't stitched a dart before, it's useful to practise these on scrap fabric beforehand.

1. On the wrong side of your fabric, you'll want to accurately mark your dart. You can use a water-soluble pen, chalk or even a basting stitch to mark the lines. If you stick a pin through the pattern at the point of the dart, you can gently pull back the pattern and mark where the pin enters the fabric. Then you can use a ruler and your marking tool to mark the rest of the dart. If you cut the pattern piece on the fold, remember to mark the dart on the other side of the pattern at the same time.

2. Fold the dart so the right sides of the fabric are brought together and match up the lines as closely as possible. Pin the dart to keep it in place, if you're using lightweight fabric, you'll want to use several pins to avoid anything slipping around.

3. Start sewing the dart from the side seam and work your way inwards towards the tip. Once you get a stitch away from the tip, stop sewing and leave long thread tails.

4. Tie a knot at the tip of the dart to secure the stitches, then press the dart with steam. You may need to use a tailor's ham to allow the fabric to curve when pressing.

Sewing Tip

Try decreasing your stitch length the closer you get to the tip of
your dart to create super secure. stitches.

HOW TO SEW A SIDE SLIT

Side slits are long, narrow openings that appear at the bottom of a side seam. In skirts, they allow for more movement when walking and can add a stylish and comfy touch to any garment. On your tops you can go for short slits at the hem (adding ease across the belly) while for your skirts you can go for thigh-high slits for a saucy look! They're super easy to sew and can transform any garment. You'll find side slits in patterns in this book, but you can easily modify any dress, skirt or top to include this detail.

1. Whatever garment you want to add the side slit to, you'll need to first finish the raw edge of the side seam with an overlocker/serger or zigzag stitch.

2. Decide how high you want your side slit to start, then mark this measurement on your side seam. Sew the seam using a ⅜in (1cm) seam allowance from the top edge down until you reach your mark.

3. Press the seam open and use a tailor's clapper to set the seam in place if using bulky fabric.

4. Fold the rest of the seam that hasn't been sewn yet towards the wrong side by ⅜in (1cm) and press in place. Use pins to secure these hems.

5. Starting from the bottom hem, sew close to the edge up the side of the slit, then pivot when you reach the end of the sewn section of the seam, sew horizontally across the seam and then pivot again and sew back down to the other hem. Make sure to sew accurately and keep a consistent seam allowance.

6. Press the side slit once more for a clean, crisp finish. You can finish the bottom hem of your garment any way you prefer – I like to make a simple double-fold hem and stitch it in place (see page 38).

64   Scrunchie

68   Tie Tote Bag

74   Maxi Skirt

82   Trendy Tote Bag

86   Shirred Dress & Top

96   Camisole Top & Dress

104   Button-back Top

112   Halter-neck Dress & Top

120   Tie-front Top

130   Cover-up & Light Summer Jacket

138   Cut-out Dress

148   Stretch Midi Skirt

156   Drawstring Trousers & Shorts

168   Tank Top

176   Button-front Dress

THE PATTERNS

SCRUNCHIE

A luxurious-looking scrunchie is the perfect simple project to sew in 15 minutes! This hair accessory is an easy pattern that uses elastic to create an effortless scrunchie and when sewn in satin or crepe it gives a luxe touch. It makes the perfect gift for loved ones!

DIFFICULTY LEVEL

Beginner

MATERIALS

- 0.2yd (0.15m) of 44in (112cm) wide woven fabric or a piece of leftover fabric 21 x 4in (53 x 10cm)

- ¼in (0.6cm) or ⅜in (1cm) wide elastic

FABRIC SUGGESTIONS

Light to medium-weight woven fabric such as satin, cotton, linen, viscose, gingham or crepe.

THE PATTERNS

Print out the pdf at 100% scale and double-check that the square on the first page is 1in (2.5cm).

PATTERN LAYOUTS

Cut out the scrunchie pattern on the fold as shown in the layout.

FOLD (RIGHT SIDES OF FABRIC TOGETHER)

CUTTING GUIDE
A: Scrunchie – cut 1 on the fold from main fabric

1 JOIN THE LONG EDGES

Fold the main scrunchie piece in half lengthways with right sides together and pin the long edges. Sew along the length with a ⅜in (1cm) seam allowance, leaving a 2in (5cm) gap towards one end.

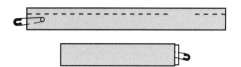

☐ RIGHT SIDE OF FABRIC

▨ WRONG SIDE OF FABRIC

2 START TO TURN THE SCRUNCHIE OUT

Take a safety pin and pierce the end of your fabric tube that is furthest away from the gap we left in the seam, then push the safety pin inside the tube as if to turn it right-side out. Pull the safety pin through until the two ends of the fabric are level and then remove the safety pin.

Sewing Tip

This is a great project for using up fabric leftover from other projects, so before you rush out and buy new, take a look through your stash to see what you can make use of.

3 JOIN THE ENDS

Now we need to join the ends so that we have a continuous ring or tube. Join the ends using a sewing machine by slowly spreading and rearranging the fabric as you sew a few stitches at a time. Alternatively, you may find it easier to sew this seam by hand.

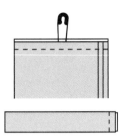

4 TURN THE SCRUNCHIE RIGHT-SIDE OUT

Turn the scrunchie to the right side by pulling the fabric through the gap we left. Once turned to the right side, I don't recommend ironing any seams as it will lose the relaxed drape of the fabric.

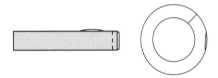

5 CUT THE ELASTIC

Wrap the uncut elastic around your wrist so it feels tight but not too restricting, then add ⅜in (1cm) to this length and cut the elastic. Pierce one end of the elastic with a safety pin.

6 INSERT THE ELASTIC

Using the safety pin, push the elastic inside the scrunchie and use your fingers to navigate it around and out the other end. When you're pushing the elastic through, make sure to keep hold of the other end! Once both ends are out, overlap them by ⅜in (1cm) and then sew over the overlap multiple times using zigzag stitch for a secure join.

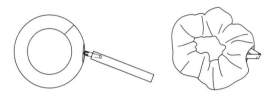

7 CLOSE THE GAP

Push the elastic and raw edges inside the scrunchie and pin the gap closed. Sew close to the edge and trim any loose threads that may have poked through to finish.

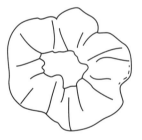

TIE TOTE BAG

This tote, with its handy inside patch pocket, is the perfect stylish accessory to add a playful touch to your outfit! You can create a tight, structured bow or a looser knot with the cute adjustable ties to suit your style. It's the perfect 30-minute make to finish off any handmade outfit.

DIFFICULTY LEVEL

Beginner

MATERIALS

• 0.85yd (0.75m) of 50in (127cm) wide woven fabric for the outer bag if using two fabrics or, if using the same fabric for both the outer and lining, you'll need just 1yd (0.9m) of fabric in total

• 0.85yd (0.75m) of 50in (127cm) wide woven fabric for the lining if using two fabrics for the bag

FABRIC SUGGESTIONS

Light to medium-weight woven fabric such as cotton, linen or gingham.

THE PATTERNS

Print out the pdf at 100% scale and double-check that the square on the first page is 1in (2.5cm). There is also an A0 pattern that you can send off to be printed if you don't want to bother with sticking all the A4/US letter pages together.

FINISHED MEASUREMENTS

Width of main bag	Height of main bag	Each strap length
9½in (24cm)	10½in (26.5cm)	13in (33cm)

PATTERN LAYOUTS

Refer to the pattern layouts for how to arrange the pattern pieces on your fabric. Note that you can either cut both the lining and outer bag from the same fabric or from two different fabrics, so follow the appropriate layout. Cut out your pattern pieces.

MAIN FABRIC | 0.85YD (0.75M)
Fabric width: 50in (127cm)

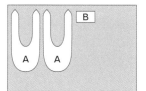

SINGLE LAYER OF FABRIC

LINING | 0.85YD (0.75M)
Fabric width: 50in (127cm)

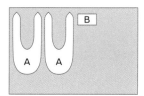

SINGLE LAYER OF FABRIC

IF USING ONLY ONE FABRIC | 1YD (0.9 M)
Fabric width: 50in (127cm)

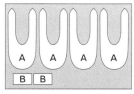

SINGLE LAYER OF FABRIC

CUTTING GUIDE
A: Main bag – cut 2 from lining and 2 from main fabric
B: Inside pocket – cut 1 from lining and 1 from main fabric

Sewing Tip

Your bag is reversible so choose a nice fabric for both the lining and outer sections and make a second patch pocket too, if you like.

1 JOIN THE POCKET PIECES

Pin the pocket pieces right sides together. Sew all round, taking a ⅜in (1cm) seam allowance and leaving a 2in (5cm) gap in the middle of the bottom edge.

☐ RIGHT SIDE OF FABRIC

☐ WRONG SIDE OF FABRIC

☐ LINING

2 FINISH THE POCKET

Clip the corners of the seam allowances on the pocket and then turn it right-side out through the gap we left. Use the blunt end of a pencil or a point turner to create sharp corners, tuck the seam allowances inside at the turning gap and then press the pocket.

3 ATTACH THE POCKET TO THE LINING

Lay out one of the lining pieces, right-side up, then place the pocket right-side up on top, with the top of the pocket 2in (5cm) from the top edge of the bag lining. Make sure the turning gap of the pocket is on the bottom edge. Pin the pocket in place and then sew close to the edge of the pocket, going down one side, across the bottom and up the other side – this will close the turning gap in the pocket at the same time.

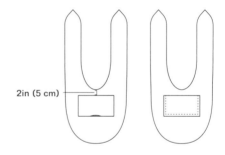

2in (5 cm)

4 SEW THE OUTER SEAM

Pin the two bag lining pieces right sides together. Sew from point to point around the outer edge with a ⅜in (1cm) seam allowance. Clip the seam allowances around the curved edges or use pinking shears to help create a smoother seam and press the edges. Repeat to join the two outer fabric pieces together.

5 JOIN THE OUTER & LINING

Keep the lining wrong-side out and turn the main fabric right-side out. Place the main fabric inside the lining and align the inner curved edges. Pin the raw edges together. Sew around the raw edges but leave a 4in (10cm) gap near the middle of the back inner curve so you can turn the bag right-side out.

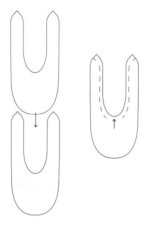

6 TOPSTITCH THE EDGES

Turn the bag right-side out through the gap we left and then push the lining inside the main bag. Tuck the seam allowances inside at the gap and then give the bag a good press, paying special attention to the top edges. Topstitch the inner top seam – this not only gives a neat, professional finish but also closes the turning gap we left. Tie a double knot to create a durable and stylish handle.

MAXI SKIRT

This slip-on skirt has a stretchy elasticated waist for comfort and two leg slits that not only give it a trendy look but add to its easy-fit styling. If you're new to dressmaking, this skirt makes a good first project as it's made from just four pieces.

DIFFICULTY LEVEL

Beginner

MATERIALS

- 2¾yd (2.5m) of 50in (127cm) wide woven fabric

- 1in (2.5cm) wide elastic – see the chart for the amount

FABRIC SUGGESTIONS

Light to medium-weight woven fabric such as viscose challis, georgette, cotton, viscose or satin.

THE PATTERNS

Print out the pdf at 100% scale and double-check that the square on the first page is 1in (2.5cm). There is also an A0 pattern that you can send off to be printed if you don't want to bother with sticking all the A4/US letter pages together.

SIZE CHART

Size	Waist	Hips
6	24in (61cm)	34in (86cm)
8	26in (66cm)	36in (91cm)
10	28in (71cm)	38in (96cm)
12	30in (76cm)	40in (101cm)
14	32in (81cm)	42in (106cm)
16	34in (86cm)	44in (111cm)
18	36in (91cm)	46in (116cm)
20	38in (96cm)	48in (121cm)
22	40in (101cm)	50in (126cm)
24	42in (106cm)	52in (132cm)
26	44in (111cm)	54in (137cm)
28	46in (116cm)	56in (142cm)
30	48in (121cm)	58in (147cm)
32	50in (126cm)	60in (152cm)

FINISHED GARMENT MEASUREMENTS

Size	Waist	Hips	Length
6		41½in (105cm)	
8		43½in (110cm)	
10		45½in (115cm)	
12		47½in (120cm)	
14		49½in (125cm)	
16		51½in (130cm)	
18	Waist is elasticated so will be fitted to you	53½in (135cm)	99cm (39in)
20		55½in (140cm)	
22		57½in (145cm)	
24		59½in (150cm)	
26		61½in (155cm)	
28		63½in (160cm)	
30		65½in (165cm)	
32		67½in (170cm)	

ELASTIC TO CUT

Size	Elastic length
6	24in (61cm)
8	26in (66cm)
10	28in (71cm)
12	30in (76cm)
14	32in (81cm)
16	34in (86cm)
18	36in (91cm)
20	38in (96cm)
22	40in (101cm)
24	42in (106cm)
26	44in (111cm)
28	46in (116cm)
30	48in (121cm)
32	50in (126cm)

PATTERN LAYOUTS

Refer to the pattern layouts for how to arrange the pattern pieces on your fabric. Cut out your pattern pieces.

ALL SIZES | 2¾YD (2.5M)
Fabric width: 50in (127cm)

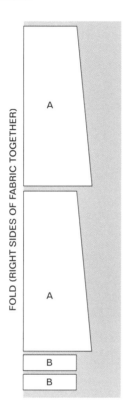

FOLD (RIGHT SIDES OF FABRIC TOGETHER)

CUTTING GUIDE
A: Front and back – cut 2 on fold from main fabric
B: Waistband – cut 2 on fold from main fabric

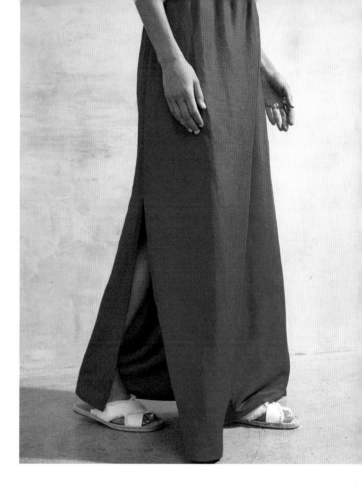

1 FINISH THE SIDE SEAMS & MARK THE SLITS

Start by finishing the raw edges of the front and back pieces down both sides using a zigzag stitch, overlocker/serger or pinking shears. Then make a mark or cut a notch to mark the top of the side slits.

2 SEW THE SIDE SEAMS

Pin and sew the side seams, taking a $^3/_8$in (1cm) seam allowance. Start at the waist and stop when you get to the notch. Press the seams open.

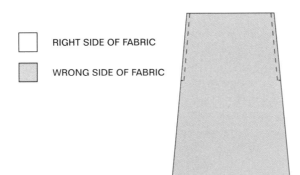

☐ RIGHT SIDE OF FABRIC

▨ WRONG SIDE OF FABRIC

3 JOIN THE WAISTBAND PIECES

Pin the waistband pieces right sides together. Sew together down each short side edge with a $^3/_8$in (1cm) seam allowance, then press open. Fold the waistband in half to bring the long edges together, with the wrong sides facing, and press to create a sharp fold at the top.

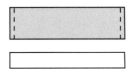

4 ATTACH THE WAISTBAND

Pin the waistband to the skirt waist edge with right sides together. First align the side seams on the waistband to the side seams of the skirt and then pin along the rest of the waist. Sew with a $^3/_8$in (1cm) seam allowance, leaving a 2in (5cm) gap at the back of the skirt so you can thread the elastic through. Press the waistband up.

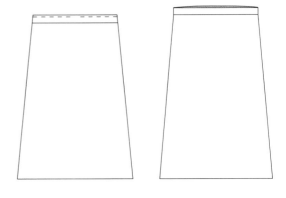

5 INSERT THE ELASTIC

Pierce one end of the elastic with a safety pin, then push it into the gap we left and navigate it around the entire waistband and out the other end. This can be a little tedious, so take your time and use your fingers to gently push and pull the elastic. Make sure you don't lose the other end of the elastic when pulling it through and don't let the elastic get twisted.

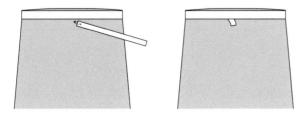

6 JOIN THE ELASTIC

Overlap the ends of the elastic by ½in (1.2cm) and then sew over the overlap multiple times using zigzag stitch for a secure join. Push the elastic inside the waistband and sew the small gap closed. Stretch the waist a few times to distribute the elastic evenly, then finish the seam using an overlocker/serger or zigzag stitch.

7 SEW THE SIDE-SLIT DETAILS

Try the skirt on and see if you like how high the leg slits are: you can extend the stitched part of the seams at this point if the slits are too high for your preference. Fold both seam allowances below the notch/slit to the wrong side by ⅜in (1cm) and pin in place. Starting at the hem edge, sew close to the edge up to the top of the slit, across and then back down to the other hem edge. Use a standard straight stitch for this. Repeat on the other side slit.

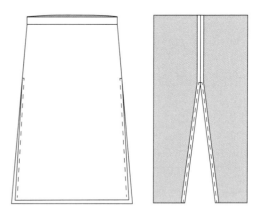

8 HEM THE SKIRT

To finish, fold the bottom edge of the skirt to the wrong side by ⅜in (1cm) and press. Fold it by ⅜in (1cm) again to enclose the raw edge and pin the hem in place. Try on the skirt to check the hem length is right for you and adjust if needed. Sew close to the edge of the hem using a straight stitch and then give your skirt a final press.

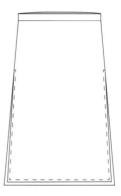

TRENDY TOTE BAG

The statement straps on this trendy tote look best when sewn in a contrasting colour. The boxy style makes it the perfect shopping bag to hold your daily essentials and brings a pop of personality to your outfit.

DIFFICULTY LEVEL

Beginner

MATERIALS

- 0.6yd (0.5m) of 50in (127cm) wide woven fabric for the main bag

- 0.5yd (0.4m) of 50in (127cm) wide woven fabric for the bag straps

FABRIC SUGGESTIONS

Medium to heavy-weight woven fabric such as cotton, cotton duck linen, corduroy, canvas or denim.

THE PATTERNS

For this pattern, you don't need to print the pdf at all. Instead, cut two pieces 13 x 16½in (33 x 42cm) for the front and back pieces and four pieces 3½ x 27in (8.9 x 69cm) for the straps.

Width of main bag	Height of main bag	Strap length
11½in (29.2cm)	13½in (34.2cm)	24½in (62.2cm)

PATTERN LAYOUTS

Refer to the pattern layouts for how to arrange the pattern pieces on your fabric. Cut out your pattern pieces.

BAG | 0.6YD (0.5M)
Fabric width: 50in (127cm)

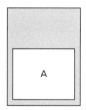

FOLD (RIGHT SIDES OF FABRIC TOGETHER)

STRAPS | 0.5YD (0.4M)
Fabric width: 50in (127cm)

FOLD (RIGHT SIDES OF FABRIC TOGETHER)

CUTTING GUIDE
A: Main bag – cut 2 from main fabric
B: Straps – cut 4 on fold from main fabric

1 JOIN THE STRAP PIECES

Pin two strap pieces right sides together and sew along one short edge with a ⅜in (1cm) seam allowance. Press the seam flat. Repeat to join the remaining two strap pieces. You now have two full-length straps, one for the front of the bag and the other for the back.

☐ RIGHT SIDE OF FABRIC

▨ WRONG SIDE OF FABRIC

2 PRESS THE STRAP EDGES UNDER

Take one strap and fold both long edges over to the wrong side of the fabric by ⅜in (1cm). Press in place. Repeat for the second strap.

3 SEW THE STRAPS

Fold each strap in half lengthways, wrong sides together and press. Topstitch close to the long edge of each strap to compete it. If you like, you can stitch along the other long edge too for symmetry, but this isn't essential.

4 HEM THE TOP OF THE BAG

Fold the top edge of one of the bag pieces over to the wrong side by 1in (2.5cm) and press. Fold by 1in (2.5cm) once more and press again. Repeat for the other bag piece, then sew close to the edge of the fold on each piece to secure the hems.

5 ATTACH THE STRAPS

Lay out one bag piece with the right side facing up. Align one end of a strap with the bottom edge of the bag piece, positioning it 3in (7.5cm) from one side edge. Pin in place. Making sure the strap isn't twisted, align the other end of the strap with the bottom edge of the bag, 3in (7.5cm) from the other side edge. Sew a rectangle to secure the strap to the bag piece, as shown, sewing over the existing stitching on the strap. Press the bag and straps. Repeat to attach the other strap to the other bag piece.

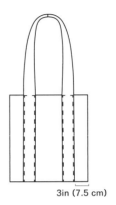

3in (7.5 cm)

6 SEW THE BAG

Pin the two bag pieces right sides together. Sew around the sides and base with a ⅜in (1cm) seam allowance. Finish the seams using an overlocker/serger, zigzag stitch or pinking shears.

7 PRESS THE BAG

Turn the bag right side and press all the seams to finish.

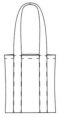

SHIRRED DRESS & TOP

This shirred pattern can be sewn as a dress or a top. It features a comfy shirred bodice that uses elastic thread and allows you to slip on the garment without tricky fastenings. The dress has a midi-length finish that includes a gathered ruffle.

DIFFICULTY LEVEL

Intermediate

MATERIALS

- **Dress:** For sizes 6–14 you'll need 3.3yd (3m) of 45–50in (114–127cm) wide woven fabric and for all other sizes you'll need 3.8yd (3.5m) of 45in (114cm) wide woven fabric

- **Top:** 1.7yd (1.5m) of 45–50in (114–127cm) wide woven fabric (all sizes)

- 1–2 reels of shirring elastic (dependent on your garments's size)

FABRIC SUGGESTIONS

Light to medium-weight woven fabric such as cotton, linen, viscose, gingham, satin or crepe.

THE PATTERNS

Print out the pdf at 100% scale and double-check that the square on the first page is 1in (2.5cm). There is also an A0 pattern that you can send off to be printed if you don't want to bother with sticking all the A4/US letter pages together.

* IF SEWING THE TOP VERSION, ONLY PRINT PAGES 1–10 *

SIZE CHART

Size	Bust	Waist	Hips
6	31in (79cm)	24in (61cm)	34in (86cm)
8	33in (84cm)	26in (66cm)	36in (91cm)
10	35in (89cm)	28in (71cm)	38in (96cm)
12	37in (94cm)	30in (76cm)	40in (101cm)
14	39in (99cm)	32in (81cm)	42in (106cm)
16	41in (104cm)	34in (86cm)	44in (111cm)
18	43in (109cm)	36in (91cm)	46in (116cm)
20	45in (114cm)	38in (96cm)	48in (121cm)
22	47in (119cm)	40in (101cm)	50in (126cm)
24	49in (124cm)	42in (106cm)	52in (132cm)
26	51in (129cm)	44in (111cm)	54in (137cm)
28	53in (134cm)	46in (116cm)	56in (142cm)
30	55in (139cm)	48in (121cm)	58in (147cm)
32	57in (144cm)	50in (126cm)	60in (152cm)

FINISHED GARMENT MEASUREMENTS

Size	Bust	Waist	Hips	Top length	Dress length
6			48in (121cm)		
8			50in (126cm)		
10			52in (132cm)	8½in (21cm)	
12			54in (137cm)		
14			56in (142cm)		
16			58in (147cm)		
18	Bust is shirred so will be fitted to you	Waist is shirred so will be fitted to you	60in (152cm)		43in (109cm)
20			62in (157cm)	9½in (24cm)	
22			64in (162cm)		
24			66in (167cm)		
26			68in (172cm)		
28			70in (177cm)	10½in (26cm)	
30			72in (182cm)		
32			74in (187cm)		

PATTERN LAYOUTS

Refer to the pattern layouts for how to arrange the
pattern pieces on your fabric. Cut out your pattern pieces.

DRESS | SIZES 6–14 | 3.3YD (3M)
Fabric width: 45in (114cm)

SINGLE LAYER OF FABRIC

FOLD (RIGHT
SIDES OF
FABRIC
TOGETHER)

DRESS | SIZES 6–24 | 3.3YD (3M)
Fabric width: 50in (127cm)

SINGLE LAYER OF FABRIC

FOLD (RIGHT
SIDES OF
FABRIC
TOGETHER)

TOP | ALL SIZES | 1YD (0.9M)
Fabric width: 45–50in (114–127cm)

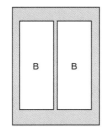

SINGLE LAYER OF FABRIC

CUTTING GUIDE
Applies to all sizes

A: Bodice – cut 2 from main fabric
B: Skirt ruffle – cut 2 on the fold from main fabric
   (if your fabric is too narrow cut 4 not on the fold)
C: Straps – cut 4 from main fabric

DRESS | ALL SIZES | 3.8YD (3.5M)
Fabric width: 45in (114cm)

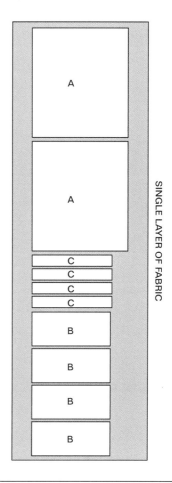

SINGLE LAYER OF FABRIC

TOP WITH STRAPS | ALL SIZES | 1.7 YD (1.5M)
Fabric width: 45–50in (114–127cm)

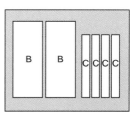

SINGLE LAYER OF FABRIC

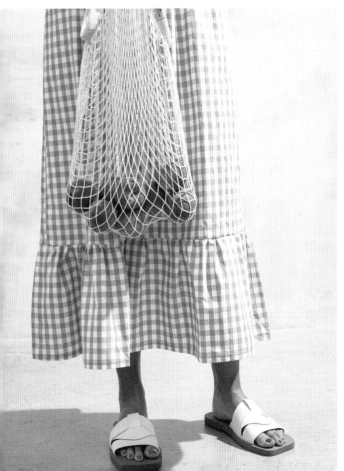

1 HEM THE TOP EDGE

The dress and top are made in the same way except when directed otherwise. To finish the top of your garment, fold the top edge of one bodice/front piece to the wrong side by ⅜in (1cm) and press. Fold the edge over again by ⅜in (1cm) and pin in place. Sew close to the edge and then press. Repeat for the other bodice piece. If you are making the top rather than the dress, hem the bottom edges of the bodice pieces in the same way.

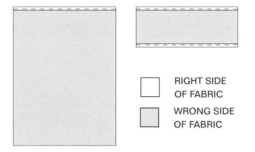

☐ RIGHT SIDE
OF FABRIC

▨ WRONG SIDE
OF FABRIC

2 MARK THE SHIRRING LINES

To make the shirring easier and neater, I find it helpful to mark the stitching lines on the fabric first using a water-soluble pen or chalk. On the right side of your fabric, mark the first line ½in (1.2cm) down from the top hemmed edge of each bodice piece. Then mark the other stitching lines – the gap between each line is up to you, but I recommend either ⅜in (1cm) or ½in (1.2cm). If you space the lines ⅜in (1cm) apart, for sizes 6–16 mark 15 lines, for sizes 18–22 mark 19 lines, and for sizes 24–32 mark 23 lines.

3 SHIRR THE BODICE PIECES

Hand wind elastic thread onto your bobbin and insert into your sewing machine. Then change your stitch length to 3–4mm, set your tension to 6 or 7 and test sew the shirring on some scrap fabric. (If you need more help with shirring, see page 50.) Sew your first line of shirring with the right side of the fabric facing up and you will see the fabric start to gather. When you come to the end of your first line, pivot the fabric, sew down to the next line and then pivot again to sew across. Repeat until you have sewn all the lines of shirring. You will need to rewind your bobbin multiple times as the elastic will run out. Repeat to shirr the other bodice piece. With the right side of the bodice pieces facing up, press the shirring with steam to help shrink the elastic even further.

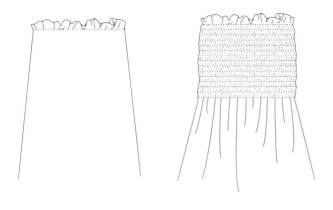

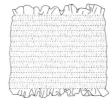

The top version will look like this

4 SEW THE SIDE SEAMS

Place the front and back pieces right sides together. Pin the side seams and sew with a ⅜in (1cm) seam allowance. Make sure you sew over the ends of the elastic rows to secure them. Finish the seam allowances using an overlocker/serger, zigzag stitch or pinking shears. Now skip to step 10 if sewing the top version.

5 JOIN THE RUFFLE PIECES

If your fabric is narrow, you will have four ruffle pieces, while if your fabric is wider, you will have two. If you have four pieces, place two of them right sides together and sew together at one side seam, taking a ⅜in (1cm) seam allowance. Repeat to join the other two pieces together. Now you have two ruffle pieces, no matter how many you started with! Place the two ruffle pieces on top of each other, right sides together, and align the side seams. Sew both these seams with a ⅜in (1cm) seam allowance. Finish the seam allowances using your preferred method. Press the seams to one side.

6 HEM THE RUFFLE

Fold the bottom edge of the ruffle to the wrong side by
⅜in (1cm) and press. Fold it again by ⅜in (1cm) and pin
in place. Sew close to the edge and then press.

7 SEW THE GATHERING STITCH

Sew a line of gathering stitches ⅜in (1cm) from the top
edge of the ruffle. To do this, start by ensuring you have
long thread tails at the start of your stitch and increase
the stitch length to 4mm. Then sew a line of stitching
along the top long edge of the front half of the ruffle
(stopping and starting the stitching at the side seams
makes the ruffle easier to attach). Don't backstitch at
the beginning or end and leave long thread tails at the
end. Repeat for the back part of the ruffle.

8 GATHER THE RUFFLE

Gently pull the bobbin thread tails to gather the ruffle
to be the same circumference as the dress. First start
gathering the front section of the ruffle and then repeat
on the back ruffle. Use your fingers to gently push the
fabric towards the middle to gather the fabric neatly.

9 ATTACH THE RUFFLE

Place the dress inside the ruffle, right sides together,
and align the side seams. Pin along the rest of the
edge and adjust the gathers to fit and appear even. Sew
using a ½in (1.2cm) seam allowance. Finish the seam
with your preferred method. Cut away any loose threads.

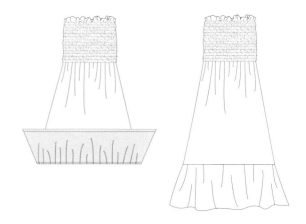

10 MAKE THE STRAPS

Take one strap and fold it in half lengthways with right
sides together. Pin and then stitch along the length and
down one end, taking a ⅜in (1cm) seam allowance.
Repeat for the other three straps.

94   SHIRRED DRESS & TOP

11 TURN THE STRAPS OUT

Clip the seam allowances at the corners of each strap and use the blunt end of a pencil to push the strap right-side out. Then use your fingers or a pointy tool to define the strap edges and press.

12 ATTACH THE STRAPS

Take a measuring tape and measure out from one side seam across the bodice front by 2½in (6cm). You want to align the open end of one of the straps to the inside of the front bodice at this point. Pin in place. Repeat with a second strap on the opposite side of the bodice front and try the dress on to see if you want to adjust the strap placement. When you're happy with the positioning, stitch the straps in place. Repeat with the remaining two straps on the bodice back.

13 TIE THE STRAPS

Tie each front strap to the corresponding back strap to create a bow. Check the fit and adjust if necessary.

CAMISOLE TOP & DRESS

A wardrobe staple, this pattern can be sewn as a top or a dress. The front neckline has a classic V-neck style while the back has a simple straight neckline. This comfy camisole slips over your head and is perfect for an evening out or dressed down with trainers.

DIFFICULTY LEVEL

Beginner

MATERIALS

• **Dress:** 3.3yd (3m) of 45–55in (114–140cm) wide woven fabric

• **Top:** 1.9yd (1.75m) of 45–55in (114–140cm) wide woven fabric

FABRIC SUGGESTIONS

Light to medium-weight woven fabric such as cotton, linen, viscose, gingham, satin or crepe.

THE PATTERNS

Print out the pdf at 100% scale and double-check that the square on the first page is 1in (2.5cm). There is also an A0 pattern that you can send off to be printed if you don't want to bother with sticking all the A4/US letter pages together.

SIZE CHART

Size	Bust	Waist	Hips
6	31in (79cm)	24in (61cm)	34in (86cm)
8	33in (84cm)	26in (66cm)	36in (91cm)
10	35in (89cm)	28in (71cm)	38in (96cm)
12	37in (94cm)	30in (76cm)	40in (101cm)
14	39in (99cm)	32in (81cm)	42in (106cm)
16	41in (104cm)	34in (86cm)	44in (111cm)
18	43in (109cm)	36in (91cm)	46in (116cm)
20	45in (114cm)	38in (96cm)	48in (121cm)
22	47in (119cm)	40in (101cm)	50in (126cm)
24	49in (124cm)	42in (106cm)	52in (132cm)
26	51in (129cm)	44in (111cm)	54in (137cm)
28	53in (134cm)	46in (116cm)	56in (142cm)
30	55in (139cm)	48in (121cm)	58in (147cm)
32	57in (144cm)	50in (126cm)	60in (152cm)

FINISHED GARMENT MEASUREMENTS

Size	Bust	Waist	Hips
6	33in (84cm)	32in (81cm)	39½in (100cm)
8	35in (89cm)	34in (86cm)	41½in (105cm)
10	37in (94cm)	36in (91cm)	43½in (110cm)
12	39in (99cm)	38in (96cm)	45½in (115cm)
14	41in (104cm)	40in (101cm)	47½in (120cm)
16	43in (109cm)	42in (106cm)	49½in (125cm)
18	45in (114cm)	44in (111cm)	51½in (130cm)
20	47in (119cm)	46in (116cm)	53½in (135cm)
22	49in (124cm)	48in (121cm)	55½in (140cm)
24	51in (129cm)	50in (126cm)	57½in (145cm)
26	53in (134cm)	52in (132cm)	59½in (150cm)
28	55in (139cm)	54in (137cm)	61½in (155cm)
30	57in (144cm)	56in (142cm)	63½in (160cm)
32	59in (149cm)	58in (147cm)	65½in (165cm)

CUTTING GUIDE
Applies to all sizes

A: Bodice front – cut 1 on fold from main fabric
B: Back bodice – cut 1 on the fold from main fabric
C: Front bodice lining – cut 1 on the fold from lining
D: Back bodice lining – cut 1 on the fold from lining
E: Straps – cut 2 from main fabric

PATTERN LAYOUTS

Refer to the pattern layouts for how to arrange the pattern pieces on your fabric. The layout assumes you will cut your lining from main fabric, but if you prefer, you can cut these pieces from a lighter weight fabric. Cut out your pattern pieces.

DRESS | ALL SIZES | 3.3YD (3M)
Fabric width: 45–55in (114–140cm)

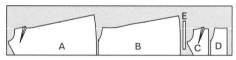

FOLD (RIGHT SIDES OF FABRIC TOGETHER)

TOP | ALL SIZES | 1.9YD (1.75M)
Fabric width: 45–55in (114–140cm)

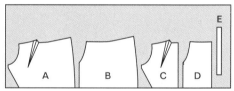

FOLD (RIGHT SIDES OF FABRIC TOGETHER)

1 MARK THE DARTS ON THE FABRIC

The top and dress are made in the same way. Use a water-soluble pen or chalk to draw the two darts on the wrong side of both the outer front and front lining pieces. (See page 58 for additional help with marking and sewing darts.)

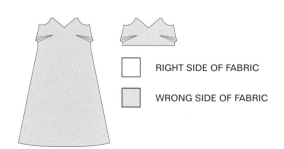

RIGHT SIDE OF FABRIC

WRONG SIDE OF FABRIC

2 SEW THE DARTS

Fold the first dart to match up the long drawn lines, right sides together. Pin in place and sew, starting from the seam edge and stitching towards the tip of the dart. Leave a long thread tail at the tip of the dart, then tie a knot to secure the threads. Press the dart upwards. Stitch all four darts in the same way.

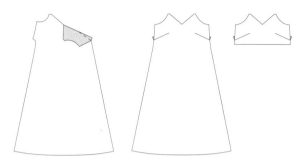

3 SEW THE SIDE SEAMS

Place the front and back pieces right sides together and pin the side seams. Sew with a ⅜in (1cm) seam allowance. Cut away the excess fabric from the dart at the raw edges and finish the seam allowances using an overlocker/serger, zigzag stitch or pinking shears. Press the seam allowances towards the back.

4 SEW THE LINING SIDE SEAMS

Place the front and back lining pieces right sides together and pin the side seams. Sew with a ⅜in (1cm) seam allowance. Cut away the excess fabric from the dart at the raw edges and finish the seam allowances as before. Press the seam allowances towards the back.

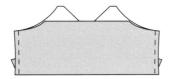

5 FINISH THE HEM OF THE LINING

Finish the raw edges of the lining at the bottom of both the front and back pieces. This can be done using an overlocker/serger, zigzag stitch or pinking shears.

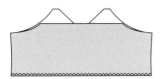

6 MAKE THE STRAPS

Fold one strap in half lengthways with right sides together and pin it. Sew along the length with a ⅜in (1cm) seam allowance. Turn the strap right-side out and press (see page 56 for help with this). Repeat to make the second strap.

7 POSITION THE STRAPS

Lay out the dress/top in front of you with the right side of the fabric facing up. Now align one end of a strap to each of the shoulder points at the front neckline. You can either baste/tack these in place or keep them secure with pins, but if using pins, make sure the pins will be out of the way of the stitching in the next step.

8 STITCH THE NECKLINE & ARMHOLES

Slide the lining over the outer dress/top so the two pieces are right sides together and the straps are sandwiched in between the fabric and the lining. Pin the layers together around the neckline and armhole edges and sew, taking a ⅜in (1cm) seam allowance but leaving a ¾in (2cm) gap in the stitching where each of the back straps will sit at the notches.

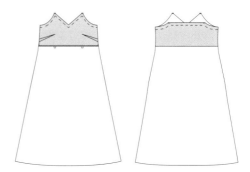

9   CLIP & TURN

Once sewn, clip the neckline and armhole seam allowances and the centre front 'V'. Turn the garment to the right side by tugging the straps and pushing the lining inside.

10   FINISH ATTACHING THE STRAPS

With the back of the dress/top right-side up, push the end of each strap ³⁄₈in (1cm) inside the appropriate gap left in step 8. Make sure the straps are not twisted and sew the gaps closed using a ³⁄₈in (1cm) seam allowance.

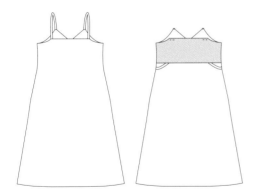

11   UNDERSTITCH THE LINING

Press the neckline and armholes. Depending on how well your fabric presses, you might want to understitch the neckline and armholes to prevent the lining from rolling out. Open the front armhole out with the right sides of the fabric facing you. Push the seam allowance of the armhole towards the lining and sew a line of stitching close to the edge of the armhole on the lining fabric, catching the seam allowances underneath to keep them from moving. You will not be able to go all the way into the armhole so just sew until you can go no further. Press for a neat finish and repeat on the other armhole and on the neckline.

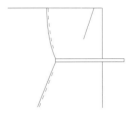

12   HEM TO FINISH

Fold the bottom edge of the top or dress to the wrong side by ³⁄₈in (1cm) and press. Fold it again by ³⁄₈in (1cm), enclosing the raw edge, and press again. Pin and then sew the hem in place, close to the edge. Press once more to finish.

BUTTON-BACK TOP

This button-back top is the perfect cropped top to throw on as part of a co-ord set. It features a simple square neckline with wide straps for comfort and there's a facing around the top and back edges for a neat, professional finish. It has a fitted bust and boxy waist for a trendy look. Try pairing this top with the drawstring trousers/pants or shorts pattern.

DIFFICULTY LEVEL

Intermediate

MATERIALS

- 1.1yd (1m) of 45–50in (114–127cm) wide woven fabric

- 0.85yd (0.75m) of 35in (89cm) wide lightweight woven interfacing

- Four ¾in (2cm) buttons

FABRIC SUGGESTIONS

Light to medium-weight woven fabric such as cotton, linen, viscose or crepe.

THE PATTERNS

Print out the pdf at 100% scale and double-check that the square on the first page is 1in (2.5cm). There is also an A0 pattern that you can send off to be printed if you don't want to bother with sticking all the A4/US letter pages together.

SIZE CHART

Size	Bust	Waist
6	31in (79cm)	24in (61cm)
8	33in (84cm)	26in (66cm)
10	35in (89cm)	28in (71cm)
12	37in (94cm)	30in (76cm)
14	39in (99cm)	32in (81cm)
16	41in (104cm)	34in (86cm)
18	43in (109cm)	36in (91cm)
20	45in (114cm)	38in (96cm)
22	47in (119cm)	40in (101cm)
24	49in (124cm)	42in (106cm)
26	51in (129cm)	44in (111cm)
28	53in (134cm)	46in (116cm)
30	55in (139cm)	48in (121cm)
32	57in (144cm)	50in (126cm)

FINISHED GARMENT MEASUREMENTS

Size	Bust	Waist
6	32in (81cm)	31½in (80cm)
8	34in (86cm)	33½in (85cm)
10	36in (91cm)	35½in (90cm)
12	38in (96cm)	37½in (95cm)
14	40in (101cm)	39½in (100cm)
16	42in (106cm)	41½in (105cm)
18	44in (111cm)	43½in (110cm)
20	46in (116cm)	45½in (115cm)
22	48in (121cm)	47½in (120cm)
24	50in (126cm)	49½in (125cm)
26	52in (132cm)	51½in (130cm)
28	54in (137cm)	53½in (135cm)
30	56in (142cm)	55½in (140cm)
32	58in (147cm)	57½in (145cm)

PATTERN LAYOUTS

Refer to the pattern layouts for how to arrange the pattern pieces on your fabric and interfacing. Cut out your pattern pieces.

FABRIC | ALL SIZES | 1.1YD (1M)
Fabric width: 45–50in (114–127cm)

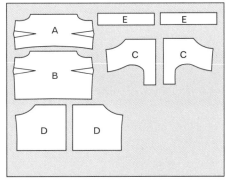

SINGLE LAYER OF FABRIC

INTERFACING | ALL SIZES | 0.85YD (0.75M)
Fabric width: 35in (89cm)

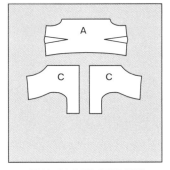

SINGLE LAYER OF FABRIC

CUTTING GUIDE
Applies to all sizes

A: Front bodice facing – cut 1 from main fabric and cut 1 from interfacing
B: Front bodice – cut 1 from main fabric
C: Back bodice facing – cut 2 (mirror) from interfacing and cut 2 (mirror) from main fabric
D: Back bodice – cut 2 (mirror) from main fabric
E: Straps – cut 2 from main fabric

1 FUSE ON THE INTERFACING

Fuse interfacing to the wrong sides of the front and back bodice facings, following the manufacturer's instructions.

2 MARK THE DARTS ON THE FABRIC

On the wrong side of the front bodice and front bodice facing, use a water-soluble pen or chalk to draw the darts. (See page 58 for additional help with marking and sewing darts.)

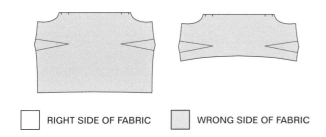

	RIGHT SIDE OF FABRIC		WRONG SIDE OF FABRIC

3 SEW THE DARTS

Fold the first dart to match up the long drawn lines, right sides together. Pin in place and sew, starting from the seam edge and stitching towards the tip of the dart. Leave a long thread tail at the tip of the dart, then tie a knot to secure the threads. Press the dart down. Stitch all four darts in the same way.

4 JOIN THE FACINGS

With right sides together, place the back bodice facings on top of the front bodice facing and pin the short straight side seams. Sew with a ⅜in (1cm) seam allowance. Cut away the excess fabric from the darts at the raw edges and finish the seam allowances using an overlocker/serger, zigzag stitch or pinking shears. Press the seam allowances towards the back.

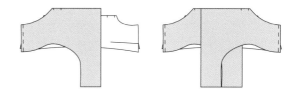

5 SEW THE MAIN SIDE SEAMS

With right sides together, place the back bodice pieces on top of the front bodice and pin the side seams. Sew with a ⅜in (1cm) seam allowance. Cut away the excess fabric from the darts at the raw edges and finish the seam allowances using an overlocker/serger, zigzag stitch or pinking shears. Press the seam allowances towards the back.

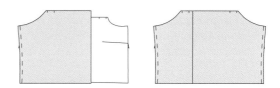

6 FINISH THE RAW EDGES

On the facing pieces, finish the lower raw edges as shown, starting by working across one straight bottom edge and then going around the inner curves and finally across the other bottom edge. Finish the bottom/hem edge of the bodice as well. Use an overlocker/serger, zigzag stitch or pinking shears for this.

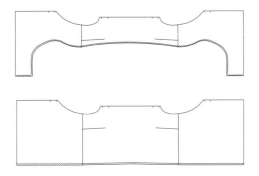

7 MAKE THE STRAPS

Fold one strap in half lengthways, with right sides together, and pin. Sew along the long edge with a ⅜in (1cm) seam allowance. Turn the strap right-side out and press so the seam is in the centre. Repeat for the second strap.

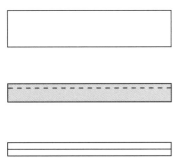

8 POSITION THE STRAPS

Lay out the bodice, right-side up, and align the strap ends with the notches at the neckline, as shown. Ensure the straps are not twisted and that the pressed centre seam of each strap is facing up. Pin the straps in place, keeping your pins well away from the seam allowance. (You can tack/baste the straps in place, if you like, to make sure they stay put.) Proceed to the next step without moving your pieces.

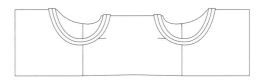

9 ATTACH THE FACING

Place the bodice facing on top of the bodice and straps, right side down, and align it along the left edge, around the neckline and armholes and along the right edge. Sew around these edges with a ⅜in (1cm) seam allowance.

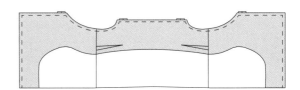

10 SEW THE BOTTOM OF THE BACK FACINGS

To achieve a clean finish, sew the bottom edge of each back facing piece right sides together with the attached back bodice, taking a ¾in (2cm) seam allowance. Stop at the edge of the facing. Clip all corners and snip into the seam allowances along the curved edges, then turn the bodice right-side out. Press all the edges.

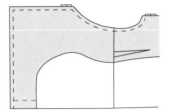

11 UNDERSTITCH THE LINING

Depending on how well your fabric presses, you might want to understitch the neckline, armholes and possibly also the centre-back edges to prevent the facing from rolling out, although the buttons and buttonholes will help hold the facing in place on the back edges. To do this, open the front bodice out around the armholes and neckline with the right sides of the fabric facing you. Push the seam allowance of the armhole towards the facing and sew a line of stitching close to the edge of the armhole on the facing, stitching through the seam allowances underneath to keep them from moving. You will not be able to go all the way into the armhole, so just sew until you can go no further. Understitch wherever possible as far as you can go and then press for a neat finish.

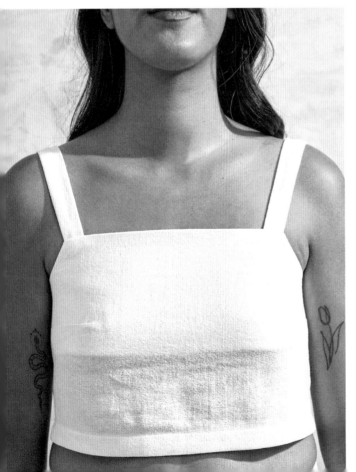

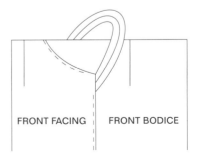

FRONT FACING   FRONT BODICE

12 STITCH THE HEM

The lower edge of the back bodice will already be finished along the section where it is attached to the facing. Press the remaining lower edge of the bodice up towards the wrong side by ¾in (2cm) – this will be in line with the seam joining the bottom of the back bodice to the facing. Sew the hem in place.

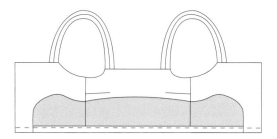

13 SEW THE BUTTONS & BUTTONHOLES

Mark four equally spaced buttonholes for your chosen buttons on the left-back bodice, positioning the top one ⅜in (1cm) from the top, the bottom one ⅜in (1cm) from the bottom edge and all of them ⅜in (1cm) from the centre-back edge of the bodice piece. The size of your buttonhole will be determined by your button size. Make sure to sew a test buttonhole on scrap fabric to see if it fits. Sew the buttonholes, then attach the buttons (see page 44) on the right-back bodice to correspond with the buttonholes. I find it easier to sew the buttonholes, align the other side underneath and then use a water-soluble pen or chalk to mark the button placements accurately.

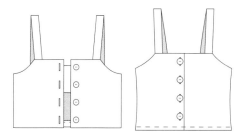

HALTER-NECK DRESS & TOP

The trendy halter-neck style of this figure-hugging midi dress features a cross-back strap design. The dress can also be sewn as a top and it just slips over your head so it's perfect for a quick change before a mid-week evening out!

DIFFICULTY LEVEL

Beginner

MATERIALS

- **Dress:** For sizes 6–18 1.8yd (1.7m) of 50in (127cm) wide stretchy fabric and for all other sizes 3.3yd (3m) of 50in (127cm) wide stretchy fabric

- **Top:** For sizes 6–18 1yd (1m) of 50in (127cm) wide stretchy fabric and for all other sizes 1.7yd (1.5m) of 50in (127cm) wide stretchy fabric

FABRIC SUGGESTIONS

Light to medium-weight stretch fabric such as viscose/jersey knits, stretch velvet or any stretchy fabric with at least 5% elastane/spandex content or at least 40% stretch.

THE PATTERNS

Print out the pdf at 100% scale and double-check that the square on the first page is 1in (2.5cm). There is also an A0 pattern that you can send off to be printed if you don't want to bother with sticking all the A4/US letter pages together.

* IF MAKING THE TOP VERSION, ONLY PRINT PAGES 1–10 *

SIZE CHART

Size	Bust	Waist	Hips
6	31in (79cm)	24in (61cm)	34in (86cm)
8	33in (84cm)	26in (66cm)	36in (91cm)
10	35in (89cm)	28in (71cm)	38in (96cm)
12	37in (94cm)	30in (76cm)	40in (101cm)
14	39in (99cm)	32in (81cm)	42in (106cm)
16	41in (104cm)	34in (86cm)	44in (111cm)
18	43in (109cm)	36in (91cm)	46in (116cm)
20	45in (114cm)	38in (96cm)	48in (121cm)
22	47in (119cm)	40in (101cm)	50in (126cm)
24	49in (124cm)	42in (106cm)	52in (132cm)
26	51in (129cm)	44in (111cm)	54in (137cm)
28	53in (134cm)	46in (116cm)	56in (142cm)
30	55in (139cm)	48in (121cm)	58in (147cm)
32	57in (144cm)	50in (126cm)	60in (152cm)

FINISHED GARMENT MEASUREMENTS

Size	Bust	Waist	Hips
6	25in (63cm)	21in (53cm)	31in (78cm)
8	27in (68cm)	23in (58cm)	33in (83cm)
10	29in (73cm)	25in (63cm)	35in (88cm)
12	31in (78cm)	27in (68cm)	37in (93cm)
14	33in (83cm)	29in (73cm)	39in (99cm)
16	35in (88cm)	31in (78cm)	41in (104cm)
18	37in (93cm)	33in (83cm)	43in (109cm)
20	39in (99cm)	35in (88cm)	45in (114cm)
22	41in (104cm)	37in (93cm)	47in (119cm)
24	43in (109cm)	39in (99cm)	49in (124cm)
26	45in (114cm)	41in (104cm)	51in (129cm)
28	47in (119cm)	43in (109cm)	53in (134cm)
30	49in (124cm)	45in (114cm)	55in (139cm)
32	51in (129cm)	47in (119cm)	57in (144cm)

There is negative ease in this pattern, so the fabric will hug your body. Go by the size chart and size down if between two sizes or grade appropriately.

PATTERN LAYOUTS

Refer to the pattern layouts for how to arrange the pattern pieces on your fabric. Cut out your pattern pieces. The lining pieces are cut from the same fabric as the outer pieces.

DRESS | SIZES 6–18 | 1.8YD (1.7M)
Fabric width: 50in (127cm)

FOLD (RIGHT SIDES OF FABRIC TOGETHER)

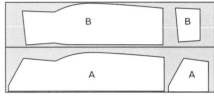

FOLD (RIGHT SIDES OF FABRIC TOGETHER)

FOLD (RIGHT SIDES OF FABRIC TOGETHER)

DRESS | SIZES 20–32 | 3.3YD (3M)
Fabric width: 50in (127cm)

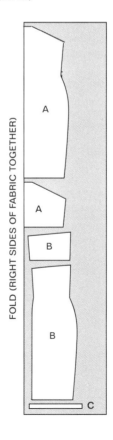

FOLD (RIGHT SIDES OF FABRIC TOGETHER)

TOP | SIZES 6–18 | 1YD (1M)
Fabric width: 50in (127cm)

FOLD (RIGHT SIDES OF FABRIC TOGETHER)

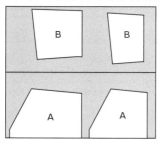

FOLD (RIGHT SIDES OF FABRIC TOGETHER)

FOLD (RIGHT SIDES OF FABRIC TOGETHER)

TOP | SIZES 20–32 | 1.7YD (1.5M)
Fabric width: 50in (127cm)

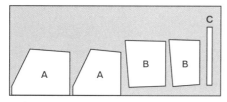

FOLD (RIGHT SIDES OF FABRIC TOGETHER)

CUTTING GUIDE
Applies to all sizes

A: Front – cut 1 on fold from lining and cut 1 on fold from main fabric
B: Back – cut 2 from lining and cut 2 from main fabric
C: Straps – cut 2 from main fabric

1 SEW THE CENTRE-BACK SEAM

The dress and top are made in the same way. Start by placing the two back pieces right sides together and pin the centre-back seam, matching the double notches. Sew, taking a ⅜in (1cm) seam allowance and using a zigzag stitch or an overlocker/serger. Press the seam and open out the pieces.

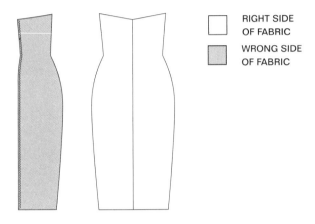

RIGHT SIDE OF FABRIC

WRONG SIDE OF FABRIC

2 SEW THE CENTRE-BACK LINING SEAM

Place the two back lining pieces right sides together and pin the centre-back seam, matching the double notch. Sew, taking a ⅜in (1cm) seam allowance and using a zigzag stitch or an overlocker/serger. Press the seam.

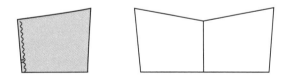

3 MAKE THE STRAPS

Fold one strap in half lengthways, right sides together, and pin. Sew, taking a ⅜in (1cm) seam allowance and using a zigzag stitch or an overlocker/serger. Turn the strap right-side out and press. Repeat for the second strap.

4 SEW THE LINING SIDE SEAMS

With right sides together, place the front and back lining pieces together and pin the side seams. Sew, taking a ⅜in (1cm) seam allowance and using a zigzag stitch or an overlocker/serger. Press the seams. It's optional to finish the bottom of the lining as knit fabric doesn't fray and it may create excess bulk.

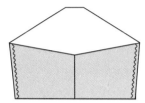

5 SEW THE MAIN SIDE SEAMS

With right sides together, place the front and back outer pieces together and pin the side seams. Sew, taking a ⅜in (1cm) seam allowance and using a zigzag stitch or an overlocker/serger. Press the seams.

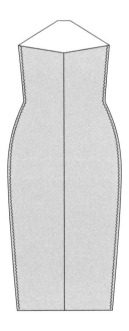

6 ALIGN THE STRAPS & LINING

Lay out the dress/top, with the right side of the front facing up, then align one end of a strap to each end of the straight part of the centre front. Pin in place. With the lining inside out, slide the lining over the top so right sides are together and the straps are sandwiched in between the outer and lining.

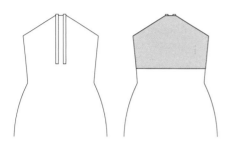

7 SEW AROUND THE TOP

Pin around the top of the dress/top. Sew the seam with a $3/8$ in (1cm) seam allowance and a zigzag stitch but leave a 1 in (2.5cm) gap where each of the straps will join to the dress back, marked by the notches.

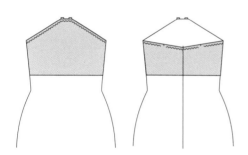

8 FINISH ATTACHING THE STRAPS

Turn the dress to the right side by tugging the straps and gently press the seam. With the back of the dress/top facing you right-side up, cross the straps and push the unfinished ends inside the gaps we left at the back by $3/8$ in (1cm). Make sure the straps are not twisted and sew the gaps closed, taking a $3/8$ in (1cm) seam allowance and using a zigzag stitch.

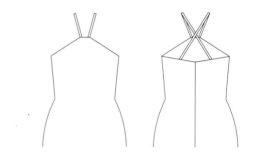

9 HEM TO FINISH

Fold the bottom edge of the dress/top to the wrong side by $3/8$ in (1cm) and press. Fold it again by $3/8$ in (1cm) and pin in place. Sew close to the edge using a zigzag stitch or twin needle, then give your finished garment a final press.

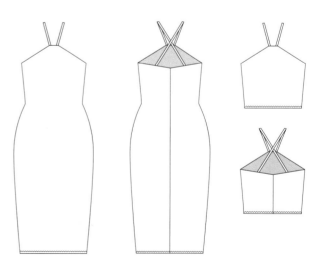

TIE-FRONT TOP

The perfect blend of cute and casual, this versatile top has a playful tie that gives a flirty touch whether you want to dress up or down! You can easily adjust the tie so the top is more fitted or looser depending on your preference. The elasticated sleeves allow for a cosy finish that looks stylish and put together. Pair this top with a maxi skirt for the perfect co-ord set!

DIFFICULTY LEVEL

Intermediate

MATERIALS

- 3.3yd (3m) of 50–55in (127–140cm) wide woven fabric

- $3/8$in (1cm) wide elastic for the sleeves – see the chart on page 122 for the amount required for each sleeve

FABRIC SUGGESTIONS

Light to medium-weight woven fabric such as cotton, linen or viscose.

THE PATTERNS

Print out the pdf at 100% scale and double-check that the square on the first page is 1in (2.5cm). There is also an A0 pattern that you can send off to be printed if you don't want to bother with sticking all the A4/US letter pages together.

SIZE CHART

Size	Bust	Waist
6	31in (79cm)	24in (61cm)
8	33in (84cm)	26in (66cm)
10	35in (89cm)	28in (71cm)
12	37in (94cm)	30in (76cm)
14	39in (99cm)	32in (81cm)
16	41in (104cm)	34in (86cm)
18	43in (109cm)	36in (91cm)
20	45in (114cm)	38in (96cm)
22	47in (119cm)	40in (101cm)
24	49in (124cm)	42in (106cm)
26	51in (129cm)	44in (111cm)
28	53in (134cm)	46in (116cm)
30	55in (139cm)	48in (121cm)
32	57in (144cm)	50in (126cm)

FINISHED GARMENT MEASUREMENTS

Size	Bust	Waist
6	33in (84cm)	30in (76cm)
8	35in (89cm)	32in (81cm)
10	37in (94cm)	34in (86cm)
12	39in (99cm)	36in (91cm)
14	41in (104cm)	38in (96cm)
16	43in (109cm)	40in (101cm)
18	45in (114cm)	42in (106cm)
20	47in (119cm)	44in (111cm)
22	49in (124cm)	46in (116cm)
24	51in (129cm)	48in (121cm)
26	53in (134cm)	50in (126cm)
28	55in (139cm)	52in (132cm)
30	57in (144cm)	54in (137cm)
32	59in (149cm)	56in (142cm)

ELASTIC LENGTH

Size	Elastic length
6	8½in (21.3cm)
8	8½in (21.8cm)
10	8¾in (22.3cm)
12	9in (22.8cm)
14	9¼in (23.2cm)
16	9½in (23.8cm)
18	9½in (24.3cm)
20	9¾in (24.8cm)
22	10in (25.3cm)
24	10¼in (25.8cm)
26	10½in (26.3cm)
28	10½in (26.8cm)
30	10¾in (27.3cm)
32	11in (27.8cm)

PATTERN LAYOUTS

Refer to the pattern layouts for how to arrange the pattern pieces on your fabric. Note that the lining for the front and back pieces is cut from the same fabric as the outer, but you can use a different fabric for the lining if you wish. Cut out your pattern pieces.

ALL SIZES | 3.3YD (3M)
Fabric width: 50–55in (127–140cm)

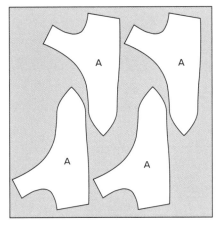

SINGLE LAYER OF FABRIC

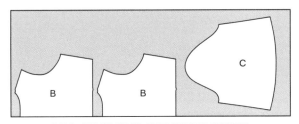

FOLD (RIGHT SIDES OF FABRIC TOGETHER)

CUTTING GUIDE
Applies to all sizes

A: Front bodice – cut 4 (2 mirror) from main fabric
B: Back bodice – cut 2 on fold from main fabric
C: Sleeves – cut 2 (mirror) from main fabric

1 MARK THE DARTS ON THE FABRIC

Use a water-soluble pen or chalk to draw all four darts on the wrong side of both the back bodice outer and back bodice lining pieces. (See page 58 for additional help with marking and sewing darts.)

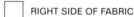

□ RIGHT SIDE OF FABRIC   ▨ WRONG SIDE OF FABRIC

2 SEW THE DARTS

Fold the first dart to match up the long drawn lines, right sides together. Pin in place and sew, starting from the seam edge and stitching towards the tip of the dart. Leave a long thread tail at the tip of the dart, then tie a knot to secure the threads. Press the dart outwards. Stitch all four darts on both pieces in the same way.

3 SEW THE SHOULDER SEAMS

Place the outer front and back bodice pieces right sides together and pin the shoulder seams. Sew with a ⅜in (1cm) seam allowance and press the seams towards the back. Repeat to join the lining pieces for the bodice back and front together.

4 ATTACH THE LINING

Lay out the outer/main pieces, rightside up, then place the lining right side down on top. Align the edges and pin the layers together. Using a ⅜in (1cm) seam allowance, stitch the layers together all round except along the side seams and armholes. Clip the seam allowances around curved edges and snip off the seam allowance at the tip of each front tie.

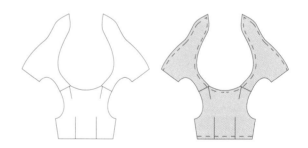

5 TURN OUT & UNDERSTITCH

Pull the top to the right side through one side edge and press the hem, front ties and neckline. Depending on how well your fabric presses, you might want to understitch the neckline and ties to prevent the lining from rolling out. To do this, push the seam allowance of the front tie towards the lining and sew a line of stitching close to the edge of the front tie on the lining fabric and through the seam allowance underneath but not stitching on the outer piece. You will not be able to go all the way into the point of the tie so just sew until you can go no further. Press for a neat finish and repeat on the other front tie and the neckline.

6 SEW THE SIDE SEAMS

The hem of the top has already been sewn, so we're going to use this to help position and sew the side seams. Open out the hem of the front bodice, flip the lining up and pin one side seam of the outer front bodice to the corresponding side seam of the outer back bodice, right sides together, and the same for the lining pieces. It will look like one long seam where the lining pieces are at one end and the main fabric pieces are at the other end. Pin and sew the side seam with a ³⁄₈in (1cm) seam allowance. Repeat for the second side seam.

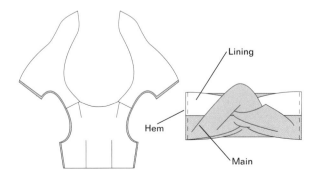

7 PRESS THE SIDE SEAMS

Flip the lining back down and pull the top to the right side through one of the armholes. Press the side seams for a flat finish.

8 SEW GATHERING STITCH

Sew a gathering stitch (see page 52) ¹⁄₄in (5mm) from the edge around each sleeve head across the top three notches. To do this, start by ensuring you have long thread tails at the start of your stitch and increase the stitch length to 2.5mm. Then sew a line of stitching around the curve of the sleeve head. Don't backstitch at the beginning or end and leave long thread tails at the end.

9 SEW THE SLEEVE UNDERARM SEAM

Fold each sleeve right sides together to align the long straight side edges and pin in place. Sew with a ⅜in (1cm) seam allowance and press the seam allowances towards the back. Open out the sleeve and gently pull the gathering stitches to create a few ripples in the fabric – use your fingers to even them out.

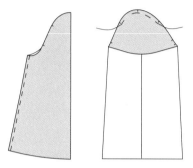

10 ATTACH THE SLEEVES

From now on, treat the bodice and bodice lining as one piece. With the bodice wrongside out and the sleeve rightside out, insert a sleeve into the bodice: the two pieces should be right sides together. Align the top of the sleeve head with the shoulder seam and align the front and back notches. Gently adjust the gathering stitches to help ease the sleeve head between the notches. Pin and sew the sleeve to the armhole with a ⅜in (1cm) seam allowance. Finish the seam using an overlocker/serger, zigzag stitch or pinking shears. Repeat to attach the second sleeve to the other armhole.

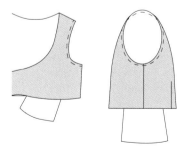

11 PRESS THE SLEEVES

Turn the top right side out and press the armholes, ensuring there are no visible gathers from the right side.

12 CREATE THE ELASTIC CASING

Fold the bottom edge of each sleeve to the wrong side by ½in (1.2cm) and press. Then fold by ½in (1.2cm) once more and pin in place. Sew close to the edge of the fold, leaving a 1in (2.5cm) gap these are all incorrectly placed in? The instructions I have show them differently with the words (fold right sides for example) please check against instructions on the back of the sleeve so you can insert the elastic. Press for a crisp finish.

13 INSERT THE ELASTIC

Pierce one end of the elastic with a safety pin and then push it into the gap in the sleeve hem and navigate it around the entire hem and out the other end. This can be a little tedious, so take your time and use your fingers to gently push and pull the elastic. Make sure you don't lose the other end of the elastic when pulling it through.

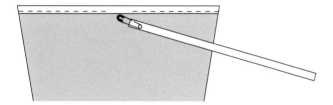

14 JOIN THE ELASTIC TOGETHER

Overlap the ends of the elastic by ⅜in (1cm) and then sew over the elastic multiple times using a zigzag stitch for a secure join. Push the elastic inside the hem and sew the small gap closed. Stretch the sleeve hem a few times to distribute the elastic and gathers evenly. Repeat to finish the second sleeve.

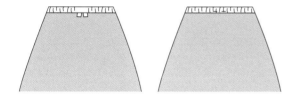

COVER-UP & SUMMER JACKET

This easy and breezy beach cover-up is the perfect addition to your holiday wardrobe. The pattern can be made as a short summer jacket that comes with a chic tie detail or as a stylish midi-length version that's perfect paired with a long dress.

DIFFICULTY LEVEL

Beginner

MATERIALS

- **Short cover-up:** For sizes 6–12 you'll need 1.3yd (1.2m) of 50in (127cm) wide woven fabric, and for all other sizes you'll need 2.2yd (2m) of 50in (127cm) wide fabric

- **Long cover-up:** 3.3yd (3m) of fabric, 50in (127cm) wide woven fabric (all sizes)

FABRIC SUGGESTIONS

Light to medium-weight woven fabric such as viscose challis, georgette, cotton, viscose or satin.

THE PATTERNS

Print out the pdf at 100% scale and double-check that the square on the first page is 1in (2.5cm). There is also an A0 pattern that you can send off to be printed if you don't want to bother with sticking all the A4/US letter pages together.

* IF MAKING THE SHORTER VERSION ONLY PRINT PAGES 1–18 *

SIZE CHART

Size	Bust	Waist	Hips
6	31in (79cm)	24in (61cm)	34in (86cm)
8	33in (84cm)	26in (66cm)	36in (91cm)
10	35in (89cm)	28in (71cm)	38in (96cm)
12	37in (94cm)	30in (76cm)	40in (101cm)
14	39in (99cm)	32in (81cm)	42in (106cm)
16	41in (104cm)	34in (86cm)	44in (111cm)
18	43in (109cm)	36in (91cm)	46in (116cm)
20	45in (114cm)	38in (96cm)	48in (121cm)
22	47in (119cm)	40in (101cm)	50in (126cm)
24	49in (124cm)	42in (106cm)	52in (132cm)
26	51in (129cm)	44in (111cm)	54in (137cm)
28	53in (134cm)	46in (116cm)	56in (142cm)
30	55in (139cm)	48in (121cm)	58in (147cm)
32	57in (144cm)	50in (126cm)	60in (152cm)

FINISHED GARMENT MEASUREMENTS

Size	Bust	Waist	Hips
6	36in (91cm)	36in (91cm)	37in (94cm)
8	38in (96cm)	38in (96cm)	39in (99cm)
10	40in (101cm)	40in (101cm)	41in (104cm)
12	42in (106cm)	42in (106cm)	43in (109cm)
14	44in (111cm)	44in (111cm)	45in (114cm)
16	46in (116cm)	46in (116cm)	47in (119cm)
18	48in (121cm)	48in (121cm)	49in (124cm)
20	50in (126cm)	50in (126cm)	51in (129cm)
22	52in (132cm)	52in (132cm)	53in (134cm)
24	54in (137cm)	54in (137cm)	55in (139cm)
26	56in (142cm)	56in (142cm)	57in (144cm)
28	58in (147cm)	58in (147cm)	(59in (149cm)
30	60in (152cm)	60in (152cm)	61in (154cm)
32	62in (157cm)	62in (157cm)	63in (160cm)

PATTERN LAYOUTS

Refer to the pattern layouts for how to arrange the pattern pieces on your fabric. Cut out your pattern pieces. The front ties can be added to either the long or short version and are optional.

SHORT COVER-UP | SIZES 6–12 | 1.3YD (1.2M)
Fabric width: 50in (127cm)

FOLD (RIGHT SIDES OF FABRIC TOGETHER)

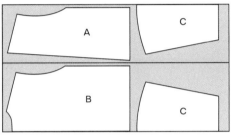

FOLD (RIGHT SIDES OF FABRIC TOGETHER)   FOLD (RIGHT SIDES OF FABRIC TOGETHER)

SHORT COVER-UP | ALL SIZES | 2.2YD (2M)
Fabric width: 50in (127cm)

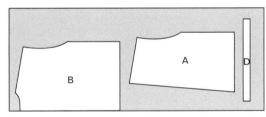

FOLD (RIGHT SIDES OF FABRIC TOGETHER)

FOLD (RIGHT SIDES OF FABRIC TOGETHER)

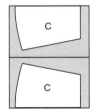

FOLD (RIGHT SIDES OF FABRIC TOGETHER)

LONG COVER-UP | ALL SIZES | 3.3YD (3M)
Fabric width: 50in (127cm)

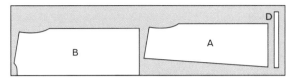

FOLD (RIGHT SIDES OF FABRIC TOGETHER)

FOLD (RIGHT SIDES OF FABRIC TOGETHER)

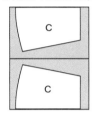

FOLD (RIGHT SIDES OF FABRIC TOGETHER)

CUTTING GUIDE
Applies to all sizes

A: Front bodice – cut 2 (mirror) from main fabric
B: Back bodice – cut 1 on fold from main fabric
C: Sleeves – cut 2 on the fold from main fabric
D: Optional front tie – cut 2 from main fabric

1 SEW THE SHOULDER SEAMS

Both the long and short cover-ups are made in the same way. Place both front bodice pieces right sides together with the back bodice and align at the shoulders. Sew the shoulder seams with a ⅜in (1cm) seam allowance. Finish the seam allowances using an overlocker/serger, zigzag stitch or pinking shears.

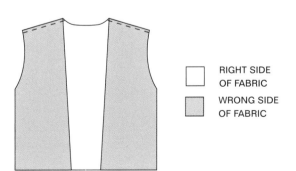

☐ RIGHT SIDE OF FABRIC

▨ WRONG SIDE OF FABRIC

2 MARK THE SLEEVE-HEAD NOTCHES

Open out the sleeves that have been cut on the fold and cut a small ¼in (0.5cm) notch at the top where the fold was to mark the middle of the sleeve head – make sure your notch stays within the seam allowance. This notch will make the next step easier.

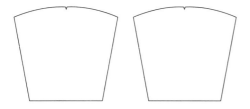

3 ATTACH THE SLEEVES

Open the bodice out so it's lying flat with the right side facing up. With right sides together, align the centre notch of one sleeve head to the shoulder seam at the armhole. Pin the rest of the sleeve head to the armhole and sew the seam, taking a ³⁄₈in (1cm) seam allowance. Finish the seam allowances using an overlocker/serger, zigzag stitch or pinking shears. Repeat to attach the other sleeve.

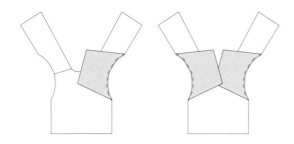

4 SEW THE SIDE & UNDERARM SEAMS

Now arrange the pieces as shown, with the sleeves folded right sides together to match the long straight edges and the front bodice pieces right sides together with the back bodice and aligned at the side edges. Pin these seams. Sew the underarm and side seams with a ³⁄₈in (1cm) seam allowance. It's easiest to start at the sleeve hem, sew up the sleeve and continue on down the side seam in one swoop around and down to the main hem edge. Finish the seam allowances using an overlocker/serger, zigzag stitch or pinking shears.

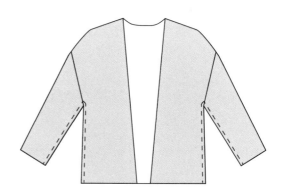

5 HEM THE FRONT/NECKLINE

Fold the front and back neckline edges over to the wrong side by ³⁄₈in (1cm) and press. Fold by ³⁄₈in (1cm) again and pin all around the neckline and down the front. Sew close to the edge, then press again for a crisp finish.

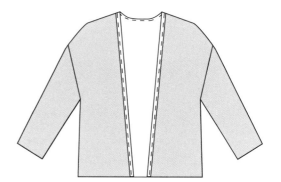

6 STITCH THE REMAINING HEMS

Fold the bottom of the garment over to the wrong side by ⅜in (1cm) and press. Fold again, this time by 1in (2.5cm), and press once more before pinning in place. Sew close to the edge and press again. Repeat the same process to hem the sleeves. Your cover-up is now complete. Follow the next steps if you'd like to add the front ties.

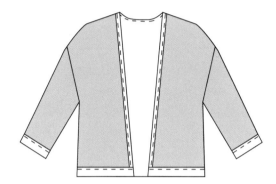

7 MAKE THE FRONT TIES

Fold one front tie piece in half lengthways, right sides together. Pin along the length and sew with a ⅜in (1cm) seam allowance. Turn it right-side out and press (see page 56 for help with this). To finish the ends of the tie, tuck them inside by ⅜in (1cm) so the raw edges are no longer visible and press flat. Sew only one of the ends closed. Repeat this step to make the other tie.

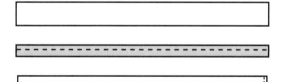

8 ATTACH THE FRONT TIES

Take a measuring tape and make a mark 12in (30cm) down from the shoulder seam on the front neckline. You want to align the unsewn end of one tie to the neckline seam at this point on the inside of the garment. Pin in place and sew the tie close to the edge, following the existing neckline stitching. You can sew over this seam multiple times to secure the tie or sew a second line parallel to this. Repeat to attach the second tie to the other front bodice and tie a bow to your liking.

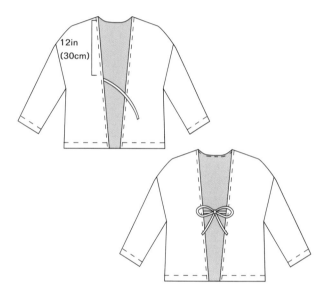

CUT-OUT DRESS

Stretchy and comfortable, this midi-length dress has a statement cut out. The neckline, bottom edge of the bodice and the top of the skirt are sewn with elastic to create a close fit that feels comfy and looks stylish! Wear this dress for an evening out as the perfect eye-catching outfit.

DIFFICULTY LEVEL

Intermediate/Advanced

MATERIALS

- **Sizes 6–14:** 2yd (1.8m) of 50in (127cm) wide stretch fabric

- **Sizes 16–32:** 3.8yd (3.5m) of 50in (127cm) wide stretch fabric

- ¼in (6mm) wide elastic – see the chart on page 141 for the amount required for each section of the dress

FABRIC SUGGESTIONS

Light to medium-weight stretch fabrics such as viscose/cotton jersey knits, stretch velvet or any stretchy fabric with at least 5% elastane/spandex content or at least 40% stretch.

THE PATTERNS

Print out the pdf at 100% scale and double-check that the square on the first page is 1in (2.5cm). There is also an A0 pattern that you can send off to be printed if you don't want to bother with sticking all the A4/US letter pages together.

SIZE CHART

Size	Bust	Waist	Hips
6	31in (79cm)	24in (61cm)	34in (86cm)
8	33in (84cm)	26in (66cm)	36in (91cm)
10	35in (89cm)	28in (71cm)	38in (96cm)
12	37in (94cm)	30in (76cm)	40in (101cm)
14	39in (99cm)	32in (81cm)	42in (106cm)
16	41in (104cm)	34in (86cm)	44in (111cm)
18	43in (109cm)	36in (91cm)	46in (116cm)
20	45in (114cm)	38in (96cm)	48in (121cm)
22	47in (119cm)	40in (101cm)	50in (126cm)
24	49in (124cm)	42in (106cm)	52in (132cm)
26	51in (129cm)	44in (111cm)	54in (137cm)
28	53in (134cm)	46in (116cm)	56in (142cm)
30	55in (139cm)	48in (121cm)	58in (147cm)
32	57in (144cm)	50in (126cm)	60in (152cm)

FINISHED GARMENT MEASUREMENTS

Size	Bust	Waist	Hips
6	31in (79cm)	24in (61cm)	35in (89cm)
8	33in (84cm)	26in (66cm)	37in (94cm)
10	35in (89cm)	28in (71cm)	39in (99cm)
12	37in (94cm)	30in (76cm)	41in (104cm)
14	39in (99cm)	32in (81cm)	43in (109cm)
16	41in (104cm)	34in (86cm)	45in (114cm)
18	43in (109cm)	36in (91cm)	47in (119cm)
20	45in (114cm)	38in (96cm)	49in (124cm)
22	47in (119cm)	40in (101cm)	51in (129cm)
24	49in (124cm)	42in (106cm)	53in (134cm)
26	51in (129cm)	44in (111cm)	55in (139cm)
28	53in (134cm)	46in (116cm)	57in (144cm)
30	55in (139cm)	48in (121cm)	59in (149cm)
32	57in (144cm)	50in (126cm)	61in (154cm)

ELASTIC LENGTHS

Size	Front Neckline	Back Neckline	Bodice Waist	Front Skirt Curve	Back Skirt Waist
6	18¾in (47.5cm)	7½in (19.3cm)	24in (61cm)	11in (27.9cm)	10½in (26.6cm)
8	19in (48.2cm)	7¾in (19.8cm)	26in (66cm)	11½in (29.2cm)	11½in (29.2cm)
10	19¼in (49cm)	8in (20.3cm)	28in (71cm)	12in (30.4cm)	12½in (31.7cm)
12	19½in (49.7cm)	8¼in (20.8cm)	30in (76cm)	12½in (31.7cm)	13½in (34.2cm)
14	20in (50.5cm)	8½in (21.3cm)	32in (81cm)	13in (33cm)	14½in (36.8cm)
16	20¼in (51.3cm)	8½in (21.8cm)	34in (86cm)	13½in (34.2cm)	15½in (39.3cm)
18	20½in (52cm)	8¾in (22.3cm)	36in (91cm)	14in (35.5cm)	16½in (41.9cm)
20	20¾in (52.8cm)	9in (22.8cm)	38in (96cm)	14½in (36.8cm)	17½in (44.4cm)
22	21in (53.5cm)	9¼in (23.3cm)	40in (101cm)	15in (38.1cm)	18½in (46.9cm)
24	21½in (54.3cm)	9½in (23.8cm)	42in (106cm)	15½in (39.3cm)	19½in (49.5cm)
26	21¾in (55cm)	9½in (24.3cm)	44in (111cm)	16in (40.6cm)	20½in (52cm)
28	22in (55.8cm)	9¾in (24.8cm)	46in (116cm)	16½in (41.9cm)	21½in (54.6cm)
30	22¼in (56.6cm)	10in (25.3cm)	48in (121cm)	17in (43.1cm)	22½in (57.1cm)
32	22½in (57.4cm)	10¼in (25.8cm)	50in (126cm)	17½in (44.4cm)	23½in (59.6cm)

Use ¼in (6mm) wide elastic for this dress.

PATTERN LAYOUTS

Refer to the pattern layouts for how to arrange the pattern pieces on your fabric according to your chosen size. Cut out your pattern pieces.

SIZES 6–14 | 2 YD (1.8M)
Fabric width: 50in (127cm)

FOLD (RIGHT SIDES OF FABRIC TOGETHER)

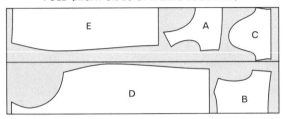

FOLD (RIGHT SIDES OF FABRIC TOGETHER)

SIZES 16–32 | 3.8YD (3.5M)
Fabric width: 50in (127cm)

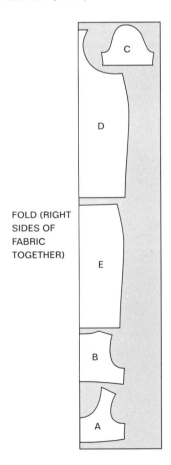

FOLD (RIGHT SIDES OF FABRIC TOGETHER)

CUTTING GUIDE
Applies to all sizes

A: Front bodice – cut 1 on fold from main fabric
B: Back bodice – cut 1 on fold from main fabric
C: Sleeves – cut 2 (mirror) from main fabric
D: Front skirt – cut 1 on fold from main fabric
E: Back skirt – cut 1 on fold from main fabric

1 SEW THE BODICE SEAMS

Pin the front bodice on top of the back bodice with right sides together and sew the shoulder and side seams with a ⅜in (1cm) seam allowance using a zigzag stitch or an overlocker/serger. Press the seams.

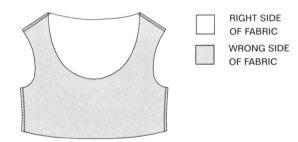

RIGHT SIDE OF FABRIC

WRONG SIDE OF FABRIC

2 ATTACH THE BACK NECK ELASTIC

Place the back bodice in front of you with the wrong side facing out. Take your back neck elastic and sew it to one shoulder seam at the neck edge with a few zigzag stitches to secure it. Then pull the elastic to fit the length of the back neck and sew on with a narrow zigzag stitch. The elastic is smaller than the neckline so you will need to stretch it out evenly as you sew.

3 FINISH THE BACK NECK ELASTIC

Fold the back neck edge to the wrong side to cover the elastic we've just attached. Sew close to the edge with a narrow zigzag stitch, stretching the elastic as you sew. Make sure the elastic is pushed up against the folded fabric edge to prevent any ripples when sewing.

4 MARK THE CENTRE-FRONT NECKLINE

Fold your front neck elastic in half and mark the fold with a pen at the centre point. Then fold the front bodice in half and mark the centre-front neck edge as well, with a notch or pen mark. This will make it easier to fit the elastic.

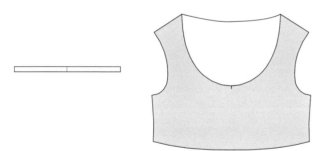

5 ATTACH THE FRONT NECK ELASTIC

Following the same method as for the back neck in step 2, we're going to sew the elastic to the front neck. This time, once you've anchored the elastic at the shoulder, stretch it to match the centre mark on the elastic with the centre mark on the neck. Stitch to that point, then adjust position and attach the rest of the elastic to the other half of the front neck. Fold the front neck edge to the wrong side to cover the elastic, just as you did in step 3, then sew close to the edge.

6 CREATE THE WAIST CASING

Fold the bottom edge of the bodice to the wrong side by ½in (1.2cm) and press. Then fold the edge by ½in (1.2cm) once more and pin along the fold. Sew close to the edge, leaving a 1in (2.5cm) gap on the back waist so you can insert the elastic. Press for a crisp finish.

7 INSERT THE ELASTIC

Pierce one end of the bodice waist elastic with a safety pin, then push it into the gap we left and navigate it around the entire hem and out the other end. This can be a little tedious, so take your time and use your fingers to gently push and pull the elastic. Make sure you don't lose the other end of the elastic when pulling it through.

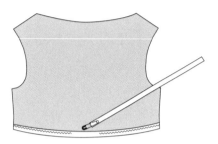

8 JOIN THE ELASTIC

Overlap the ends of the elastic by ⅜in (1cm) and then sew over the overlap multiple times using zigzag stitch for a secure join. Push the elastic inside the hem and sew the small gap closed.

9 PRESS THE BODICE

Turn the bodice to the right side and gently stretch the bottom edge a few times to evenly distribute the elastic and gathers that form. Gently press the neckline and waist edges.

10 JOIN THE SKIRT PIECES TOGETHER

Pin the back skirt on top of the front skirt with right sides together. Sew the two side seams with a ⅜in (1cm) seam allowance and a zigzag stitch or using an overlocker/serger. Press the seams.

11 SEW THE BACK SKIRT WAIST

Following the same method as for the back neck in step 2, sew the elastic to the back waist. As in step 3, fold the back waist edge to the wrong side to cover the elastic and sew close to the edge.

12 SEW THE FRONT SKIRT CURVES

Cut the front skirt elastic – the measurement provided in the chart is for each curve. As in step 4, mark the centre of your elastic and one front curve on the skirt then follow the same technique as in step 5 to stretch the elastic and sew it in place to the centre marks, then adjust the positioning and sew the rest of the curve. As before, fold the edge with the elastic attached to the wrong side and sew close to the edge. Repeat on the other front curve, then finish the top raw edge of the skirt front with a zigzag stitch or using an overlocker/ serger for a neat finish.

13 UNITE THE BODICE & SKIRT

With the right side of the bodice and skirt facing you, insert the front skirt down through the front bodice neck and align it with the bodice hem on the inside.

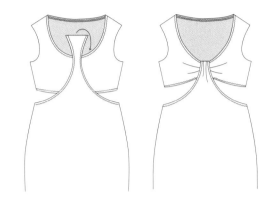

14 SEW THE FRONT CURVES IN PLACE

Look at the dress from the wrong side and pin the back of the front curve to the skirt so the bodice is now sandwiched in the middle. The overlap of the front skirt curve should measure 3½in (9cm). Follow the existing stitching lines and sew two short lines of zigzag stitches at the hem to keep the skirt in place. Make sure these stitches are secure as they are holding the skirt up!

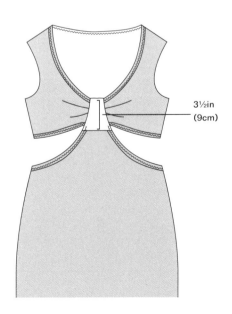

3½in (9cm)

15 SEW THE UNDERARM SEAMS

Fold each sleeve lengthways, with right sides together, and align and then pin the underarm seams. Sew the seam with a ⅜in (1cm) seam allowance, using a zigzag stitch or overlocker/serger. Press the seam.

16 HEM THE SLEEVES

Fold the bottom edge of each sleeve to the wrong side by ⅜in (1cm) and press. Pin along the hem and sew close to the edge using a narrow zigzag stitch. Press each sleeve for a crisp finish.

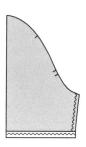

17 ATTACH THE SLEEVES

With the bodice wrong-side out and the sleeve right-side out, insert a sleeve into the armhole. Align the top of the sleeve head with the shoulder seam and match up the front and back notches. Pin and sew the sleeve to the armhole using a zigzag stitch or overlocker/serger. Press the seam. Repeat to attach the other sleeve.

18 HEM THE DRESS

Fold the bottom edge of the skirt to the wrong side by 1in (2.5cm) and press. Sew close to the edge using a zigzag stitch or twin needle, then press.

STRETCH MIDI SKIRT

This midi skirt is made from a knit fabric and features a stretchy elasticated waist for extra comfort. It has a slip-on style and a high leg slit for a trendy look. Pair this with a crop top or tuck in a camisole to create an easy yet put-together look.

DIFFICULTY LEVEL

Beginner

MATERIALS

- Sizes 6–18: 1.4yd (1.25m) of 50in (127cm) wide stretch fabric

- Sizes 20–32: 2.4yd (2.25m) of 50in (127cm) wide stretch fabric

- 1in (2.5cm) wide elastic – see the chart on page 150 for the amount

FABRIC SUGGESTIONS

Light to medium-weight stretch fabric such as viscose/jersey knits, stretch velvet or any stretchy fabric with at least 5% elastane/spandex content or at least 40% stretch.

THE PATTERNS

Print out the pdf at 100% scale and double-check that the square on the first page is 1in (2.5cm). There is also an A0 pattern that you can send off to be printed if you don't want to bother with sticking all the A4/US letter pages together.

SIZE CHART

Size	Waist	Hips
6	24in (61cm)	34in (86cm)
8	26in (66cm)	36in (91cm)
10	28in (71cm)	38in (96cm)
12	30in (76cm)	40in (101cm)
14	32in (81cm)	42in (106cm)
16	34in (86cm)	44in (111cm)
18	36in (91cm)	46in (116cm)
20	38in (96cm)	48in (121cm)
22	40in (101cm)	50in (126cm)
24	42in (106cm)	52in (132cm)
26	44in (111cm)	54in (137cm)
28	46in (116cm)	56in (142cm)
30	48in (121cm)	58in (147cm)
32	50in (126cm)	60in (152cm)

FINISHED GARMENT MEASUREMENTS

Size	Waist	Hips	Length
6		36in (91cm)	
8		38in (96cm)	
10		40in (101cm)	
12		42in (106cm)	
14		44in (111cm)	
16		46in (116cm)	
18	Waist is elasticated so will be fitted to you	48in (121cm)	36in (91cm)
20		50in (126cm)	
22		52in (132cm)	
24		54in (137cm)	
26		56in (142cm)	
28		58in (147cm)	
30		60in (152cm)	
32		62in (157cm)	

ELASTIC TO CUT

Size	Elastic length
6	24in (61cm)
8	26in (66cm)
10	28in (71cm)
12	30in (76cm)
14	32in (81cm)
16	34in (86cm)
18	36in (91cm)
20	38in (96cm)
22	40in (101cm)
24	42in (106cm)
26	44in (111cm)
28	46in (116cm)
30	48in (121cm)
32	50in (126cm)

Use 1in (2.5cm) wide elastic for the waist.

PATTERN LAYOUTS

Refer to the pattern layouts for how to arrange the pattern pieces on your fabric. Cut out your pattern pieces.

SIZES 6–18 | 1.4 YD (1.25M)
Fabric width: 50in (127cm)

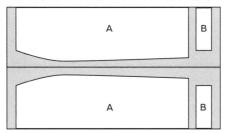

FOLD (RIGHT SIDES OF FABRIC TOGETHER)

FOLD (RIGHT SIDES OF FABRIC TOGETHER)

SIZES 20–32 | 2.4 YD (2.25M)
Fabric width: 50in (127cm)

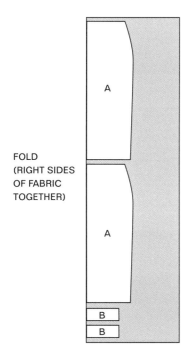

FOLD (RIGHT SIDES OF FABRIC TOGETHER)

CUTTING GUIDE
Applies to all sizes

A: Front and back – cut 2 on fold from main fabric
B: Waistband – cut 2 on fold from main fabric

1 MARK THE SIDE SLIT

This skirt pattern has a side slit detail that can be sewn on the right or the left side – or on both sides. Decide which option you'd like to choose and make a mark or cut a notch for the side slit.

2 SEW THE FIRST SIDE SEAM

Place the two skirt pieces right sides together. Pin and sew the side seam without the side-slit detail, taking a ⅜in (1cm) seam allowance. Make sure to use a zigzag stitch or an overlocker/serger so the seam will stretch with the fabric. Press the seam.

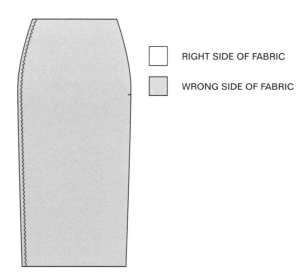

☐ RIGHT SIDE OF FABRIC

▨ WRONG SIDE OF FABRIC

3 SEW THE OTHER SIDE SEAM

Pin and sew the side seam with the side slit, taking a $\frac{3}{8}$in (1cm) seam allowance and using a zigzag stitch, not an overlocker/serger for this step. Start from the waist and stop when you get to the notch that marks the top of the slit. Press the seam.

4 JOIN THE WAISTBAND PIECES

Pin the waistband pieces right sides together and sew both short side seams, taking a $\frac{3}{8}$in in (1cm) seam allowance and using a zigzag stitch or an overlocker/serger. Fold the waistband in half, with the wrong sides together and press to create a sharp fold at the top of the waistband.

5 ATTACH THE WAISTBAND

With right sides together, pin the waistband to the skirt's waist edge. First align the side seams and then pin along the rest of the waist. Sew with a $\frac{3}{8}$in (1cm) seam allowance, using a zigzag stitch or an overlocker/serger and leaving a 2in (5cm) gap at the back of the skirt so you can thread in the elastic. Press the waistband up.

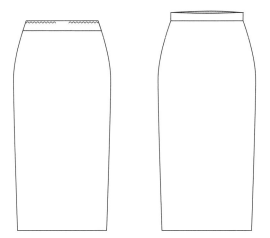

6 INSERT THE ELASTIC

Pierce one end of the elastic with a safety pin then push it into the gap we left in the waistband and navigate it around the entire thing and out the other end. This can be a little tedious, so take your time and use your fingers to gently push and pull the elastic. Don't twist the elastic and make sure you don't lose the other end of it when pulling it through!

7 JOIN THE ELASTIC TOGETHER

Overlap the ends of the elastic by ½in (1.2cm) and then sew over the overlap multiple times using a zigzag stitch for a secure join. Push the elastic inside the waistband and sew the small gap closed. Stretch the waist a few times to distribute the elastic evenly, then finish the seam using an overlocker/serger or zigzag stitch.

8 SEW THE SIDE SLIT

Try the skirt on and see if you like how high the leg slit is: you can extend the stitched part of the seam at this point if the slit is too high for your preference. Fold the side seam below the notch/slit to the wrong side by ⅜in (1cm) and pin in place. Starting at the hem, sew close to the edge up to the slit, across and then back down to the other hem. You can use a straight stitch or zigzag stitch for this.

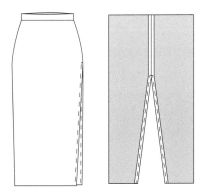

9 HEM THE SKIRT

Fold the bottom of the skirt to the wrong side by ⅜in (1cm) and press. Fold it again by ⅜in (1cm) and then pin in place. Try on the skirt to check the hem length is right for you and adjust if needed, then sew close to the edge of the hem fold using a zigzag stitch or twin needle. Press gently, making sure to use the appropriate setting on your iron.

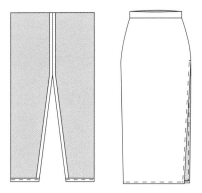

DRAWSTRING TROUSERS & SHORTS

Chic yet comfortable, this design can be made as trousers/pants or shorts. It features a drawstring detail with an elasticated waistband for a slip-on style. The wide legs and cargo pockets combine to make this a trendy wardrobe staple.

DIFFICULTY LEVEL

Intermediate

MATERIALS

- **Shorts:** 1.8yd (1.7m) of 50in (127cm) wide woven fabric

- **Trousers:** 3.3yd (3m) of 50in (127cm) wide woven fabric

- Two 1in (2.5cm) squares of woven interfacing

- 1in (2.5cm) wide elastic – see the chart for the amount

FABRIC SUGGESTIONS

Light to medium-weight woven fabric such as cotton, linen, viscose, cotton twill or corduroy.

THE PATTERNS

Print out the pdf at 100% scale and double-check that the square on the first page is 1in (2.5cm). There is also an A0 pattern that you can send off to be printed if you don't want to bother with sticking all the A4/US letter pages together.

* IF MAKING THE SHORTS VERSION ONLY PRINT PAGES 1–18 *

SIZE CHART

Size	Waist	Hips
6	24in (61cm)	34in (86cm)
8	26in (66cm)	36in (91cm)
10	28in (71cm)	38in (96cm)
12	30in (76cm)	40in (101cm)
14	32in (81cm)	42in (106cm)
16	34in (86cm)	44in (111cm)
18	36in (91cm)	46in (116cm)
20	38in (96cm)	48in (121cm)
22	40in (101cm)	50in (126cm)
24	42in (106cm)	52in (132cm)
26	44in (111cm)	54in (137cm)
28	46in (116cm)	56in (142cm)
30	48in (121cm)	58in (147cm)
32	50in (126cm)	60in (152cm)

FINISHED GARMENT MEASUREMENTS

Size	Waist	Hips	Inseam
6		36in (91cm)	
8		38in (96cm)	
10		40in (101cm)	
12		42in (106cm)	
14		44in (111cm)	
16		46in (116cm)	
18	Waist is elasticated so will be fitted to you	48in (121cm)	**Shorts** 2¾in (7cm) **Trousers** 28in (71cm)
20		50in (126cm)	
22		52in (132cm)	
24		54in (137cm)	
26		58in (142cm)	
28		58in (147cm)	
30		60in (152cm)	
32		62in (157cm)	

ELASTIC TO CUT

Size	Elastic length
6	24in (61cm)
8	26in (66cm)
10	28in (71cm)
12	30in (76cm)
14	32in (81cm)
16	34in (86cm)
18	36in (91cm)
20	38in (96cm)
22	40in (101cm)
24	42in (106cm)
26	44in (111cm)
28	46in (116cm)
30	48in (121cm)
32	50in (126cm)

Use 1in (2.5cm) wide elastic for the waist.

PATTERN LAYOUTS

Refer to the pattern layouts for how to arrange the pattern pieces on your fabric. Cut out your pattern pieces.

SHORTS | ALL SIZES | 1.8YD (1.7M)
Fabric width: 50in (127cm)

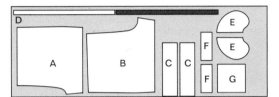

FOLD (RIGHT SIDES OF FABRIC TOGETHER)

TROUSERS | ALL SIZES | 3.3YD (3M)
Fabric width: 50in (127cm)

CUTTING GUIDE
Applies to all sizes

A: Front leg – cut 2 (mirror) from main fabric
B: Back leg – cut 2 (mirror) from main fabric
C: Waistband – cut 2 on the fold from main fabric
D: Drawstring – cut 1 on the fold from main fabric
E: Pocket bag – cut 4 from main fabric
F: Pocket flap (only for trousers) – cut 4 from main fabric
G: Cargo pocket (only for trousers) – cut 2 from main fabric

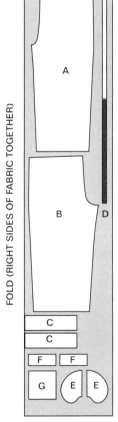

FOLD (RIGHT SIDES OF FABRIC TOGETHER)

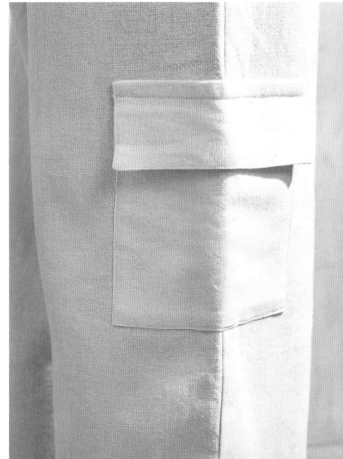

1 FINISH THE EDGES

The shorts and trousers are made in the same way except when directed otherwise. First, finish the raw edges of all four pocket bags and the side/outside leg seams of the two front and two back shorts/trouser pieces. This can be done using an overlocker/serger, zigzag stitch or pinking shears to ensure a neat finish.

2 ATTACH THE INSEAM POCKET

Place one pocket bag right sides together with the trouser/shorts front side seam, with the top of the pocket bag 1½in (4 cm) below the waist edge. Pin and sew with a ⅜in (1cm) seam allowance. Repeat for the other three trouser/shorts pieces.

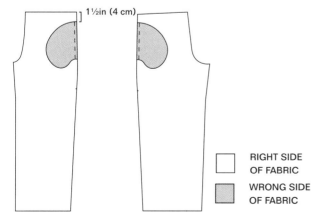

1½in (4 cm)

| | RIGHT SIDE OF FABRIC |
| | WRONG SIDE OF FABRIC |

3 UNDERSTITCH THE POCKET BAGS

To make sure that the pocket fabric doesn't show, we will do some understitching. Fold the pocket bag outwards and press flat. Stitch the pocket close to the edge of the fold, stitching through both the pocket fabric and the seam allowances. Repeat on the other three trouser/shorts pieces.

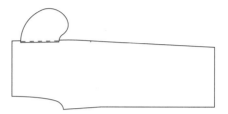

4 SEW THE POCKETS & SIDE SEAMS

With right sides together, match each front piece to the corresponding back piece and pin around the pocket bag and side seam. Sew this side seam with a ⅜in (1cm) seam allowance. Use the previous stitching as a guide on where to pivot across to the pocket and back from the pocket and on down the leg again. (See page 46 for more help on sewing inseam pockets.) Press the seams. **If sewing the shorts version, skip on to step 9.**

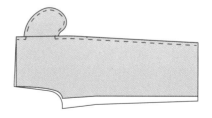

Sewing Tip

If you find you've forgotten to mark a notch or you've overlocked
over it and can't see it anymore, just take the original pattern piece
and use a tape measure to find its position so you can re-mark it.

5 PREPARE THE CARGO POCKETS

Finish all four edges of both cargo pocket pieces using an overlocker/serger, zigzag stitch or pinking shears. Now fold the top edge of each pocket (marked with a notch) towards the wrong side by 1in (2.5cm) to make a hem and press it. Stitch the pocket hem close to the edge.

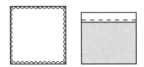

Fold the bottom pocket edge to the wrong side by ⅜in (1cm), press the fold and pin in place. Then fold the sides of the pocket in by ⅜in (1cm) and press and pin in place.

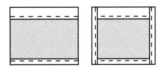

6 ATTACH THE CARGO POCKETS

Open out each trouser leg so the side seam is in the middle and the right side is facing up. Find the top middle edge of one pocket and align it with the notch on the trouser side seam. Make sure that the right side of the pocket is facing up, and that it's centred and straight.

Pin the left, bottom and right edges to the trouser leg. Sew the pocket close the edge, starting at the top right-hand corner, pivoting across the bottom and then sewing back up to the top left-hand corner. Press the pocket once sewn. Repeat for the other cargo pocket and trouser leg.

7 MAKE THE POCKET FLAPS

Pin two pocket flaps right sides together and, with a ⅜in (1cm) seam allowance, sew around the sides and one long edge – the long edge will be the bottom of the flap once it is on the trousers. Clip the corners of the seam allowances and turn the flap right-side out. Repeat to make the other pocket flap, then press both flaps.

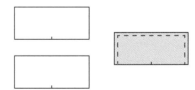

Topstitch around the three sewn edges of each pocket flap and press again.

Finish the raw edge of the bottom of the pocket flap using an overlocker, zigzag stitch or pinking shears. Repeat for the other pocket flap.

8 ATTACH THE POCKET FLAPS

Place a pocket flap $^3/_8$ in (1cm) above one pocket and on top of the trouser side seam, right sides together with the trouser leg and with the raw edges facing down towards the pocket. Make sure the flap is aligned with the pocket and then sew with a $^3/_8$ in (1cm) seam allowance. Trim the seam allowance a little then fold the pocket flap down over it and sew $^3/_8$ in (1cm) from the fold – this will enclose the seam allowances. Repeat for the other leg.

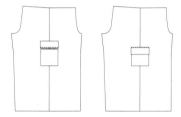

9 SEW THE INSIDE-LEG SEAMS

Fold each leg of the trousers/shorts right sides together and pin the inside leg seam. You will need to pull the front leg gently and align it with the back leg. Sew the seam with a $^3/_8$ in (1cm) seam allowance, then finish the seam allowances with your preferred method. Repeat on the other leg and press the seams.

10 SEW THE CROTCH SEAM

Turn one leg right-side out and slip it inside the other leg so they are right sides together. Align the crotch seam. Pin the entire front and back crotch curves. Sew with a $^3/_8$ in (1cm) seam allowance, then finish the seams as before.

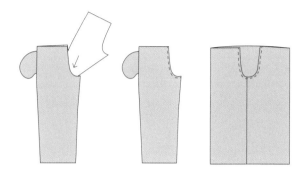

11 TURN THE TROUSERS OUT

Turn the legs right-side out to see your trousers/shorts have taken shape.

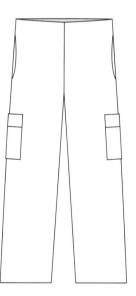

12 MAKE THE BUTTONHOLES

Take one of your waistband pieces (for the front) and mark the buttonhole openings for the drawstring cord. Iron on a small square of interfacing to the wrong side of the fabric where each buttonhole will go to strengthen the fabric. Make two ³⁄₈in (1cm) buttonholes, centring the marked lines. Don't repeat this on the other waistband piece!

13 JOIN THE WAISTBAND PIECES

Pin the waistband pieces right sides together. Sew the short side edges together with a ³⁄₈in (1cm) seam allowance. Fold the waistband in half, wrong sides together, and press to create a sharp fold at the top of the waistband.

14 ATTACH THE WAISTBAND

With right sides together, pin the waistband to the waist edge of your trousers/shorts, making sure the front of the waistband where the buttonholes are is facing the front of the trousers/shorts. First align the side seams and then pin along the rest of the waist. Sew with a ³⁄₈in (1cm) seam allowance, leaving a 3in (7.5cm) gap at the back of the trousers/shorts so you can insert the elastic. Once done, press the waistband up.

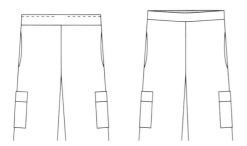

15 INSERT THE ELASTIC

Pierce one end of the elastic with a safety pin, then push it into the gap we left and navigate it around the entire waistband and out the other end. This can be a little tedious, so take your time and use your fingers to gently push and pull the elastic. Make sure you don't lose the other end of the elastic when pulling it through and don't twist the elastic.

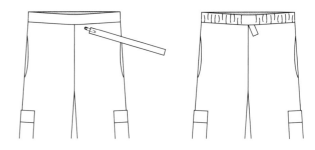

16 JOIN THE ELASTIC

Overlap the ends of the elastic by ½in (1.2cm) and then sew over the overlap multiple times using zigzag stitch for a secure join. Push the elastic back inside the waistband and sew the small gap closed. Stretch the waist a few times to distribute the elastic and gathers evenly. Finish the seam as before.

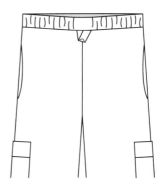

17 SEW THE DRAWSTRING CASING

Sew a line of stitching ⅜in (1cm) below the top of the waistband and parallel to the top edge. It's easier to sew the waist in sections by using one hand to hold the fabric from the back and the other hand to stretch the fabric so the waistband is taut as you sew. Make sure you are stretching the elastic as you sew to create even gathers. Repeat the same process to sew a line of stitching ⅜in (1cm) above the bottom of the waistband and parallel to the edge.

18 MAKE THE DRAWSTRING

Press each long edge of the drawstring strip to the wrong side of the fabric by ⅜in (1cm).

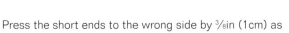

Press the short ends to the wrong side by ⅜in (1cm) as well. Fold the entire piece in half lengthways, wrong sides together, and press.

Edgestitch around the open edges, starting from the fold to stitch down one end, pivoting and sewing along the long edge and then back up the other end. Press the finished drawstring.

19 INSERT THE DRAWSTRING

Pierce one end of the drawstring with a safety pin and guide it through one buttonhole, around the waistband and out of the other buttonhole. Use your fingers to gently guide the drawstring through. Once it is out the other end, pull the drawstring ends to make them even.

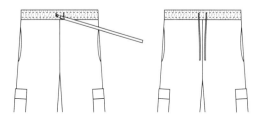

20 HEM TO FINISH

Fold the bottom edge of each leg to the wrong side by ⅜in (1cm) and press. Fold it again, this time by 1in (2.5cm), and pin along the hem. Sew close to the edge and press for a crisp finish.

TANK TOP

A key wardrobe staple, this trendy tank top is the perfect cropped top to pair with shorts or skirts. The neck and armholes are finished with narrow bands, which can be cut from a different fabric, if desired, for a pop of colour.

DIFFICULTY LEVEL

Beginner

MATERIALS

- **Sizes 6–18:** 0.9yd (0.75m) of 50–58in (127–147cm) wide stretch fabric

- **Sizes 20–32:** 1.4yd (1.25m) of 50in (127cm) wide stretch fabric or 0.9yd (0.75m) of 58in (147cm) wide fabric

FABRIC SUGGESTIONS

Light to medium-weight knit fabric such as jersey, viscose jersey, cotton jersey, ribbed knit or ponte roma.

THE PATTERNS

Print out the pdf at 100% scale and double-check that the square on the first page is 1in (2.5cm). There is also an A0 pattern that you can send off to be printed if you don't want to bother with sticking all the A4/US letter pages together.

SIZE CHART

Size	Bust	Waist
6	31in (79cm)	24in (61cm)
8	33in (84cm)	26in (66cm)
10	35in (89cm)	28in (71cm)
12	37in (94cm)	30in (76cm)
14	39in (99cm)	32in (81cm)
16	41in (104cm)	34in (86cm)
18	43in (109cm)	36in (91cm)
20	45in (114cm)	38in (96cm)
22	47in (119cm)	40in (101cm)
24	49in (124cm)	42in (106cm)
26	51in (129cm)	44in (111cm)
28	53in (134cm)	46in (116cm)
30	55in (139cm)	48in (121cm)
32	57in (144cm)	50in (126cm)

FINISHED GARMENT MEASUREMENTS

Size	Bust	Waist	Length
6	25½in (65cm)	22in (56cm)	10½in (26.5cm)
8	27½in (90cm)	24in (61cm)	10¾in (27cm)
10	29½in (75cm)	26in (66cm)	11in (27.5cm)
12	31½in (80cm)	28in (71cm)	11⅛in (28cm)
14	33½in (85cm)	30in (76cm)	11¼in (28.5cm)
16	35½in (90cm)	32in (81cm)	11½in (29cm)
18	37½in (95cm)	34in (86cm)	11¾in (29.5cm)
20	39½in (100cm)	36in (91cm)	12in (30cm)
22	41½in (105cm)	38in (96cm)	12⅛in (30½cm)
24	43½in (110cm)	40in (101cm)	12¼in (31cm)
26	45½in (115cm)	42in (106cm)	12½in (31½cm)
28	47½in (120cm)	44in (111cm)	12¾in (32cm)
30	49½in (125cm)	46in (116cm)	13in (32½cm)
32	51½in (130cm)	48in (121cm)	13⅛in (33cm)

There is negative ease in this pattern, so the fabric will hug your body.

PATTERN LAYOUTS

Refer to the pattern layouts for how to arrange the pattern pieces on your fabric, choosing the one that matches the width of fabric you have chosen. Cut out your pattern pieces.

SIZES 6–18 | 0.9YD (0.75M)
Fabric width: 50in (127cm)

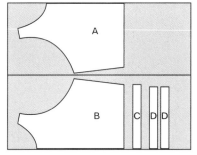

SIZES 20–32 | 1.4YD (1.25M)
Fabric width: 50in (127cm)

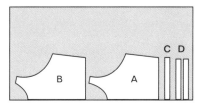

ALL SIZES | 0.9YD (0.75M)
Fabric width: 58in (147cm)

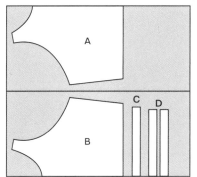

1   MARK THE CENTRE NECKLINES

Take the front and back pieces and cut a small notch at
the centre of the neckline where the fold was when you
cut each piece out, making sure you keep the notch within
the ³⁄₈in (1cm) seam allowance. This notch will make it
easier to align the neck band piece later.

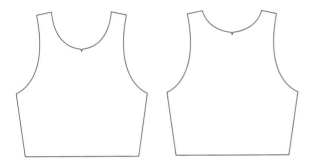

2   SEW THE MAIN SEAMS

Place the front and back pieces right sides together and
pin the shoulder and side seams. Sew with a ³⁄₈in (1cm)
seam allowance, using a zigzag stitch or an overlocker/
serger so that the stitching can stretch with the fabric.

☐ RIGHT SIDE
OF FABRIC

▨ WRONG SIDE
OF FABRIC

3 PREPARE THE NECK BAND

Fold the neck band piece in half, right sides together, to align the ends and sew the end seam with a ⅜in (1cm) seam allowance, using a zigzag stitch or an overlocker/serger. See page 54 for photo steps on how to sew a knit neckband.

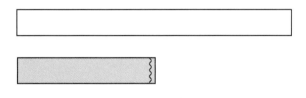

Open out the neck band: it should now form a ring. Fold the neck band in half lengthways, wrong sides together, and press the folded edge.

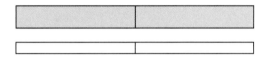

Lay out the neck band with the seam at one side, then cut or mark a notch on the other side to determine the centre.

Rearrange the band by matching this notch to the seam and now cut or mark notches at the folds to mark two quarters of the neck band.

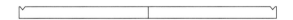

4 PIN ON THE NECK BAND

Align the centre seam of the neck band to the centre notch on the back neck of the tank, making sure that right sides and raw edges are together. Then align the opposite neck band notch with the centre notch on the front neckline and the remaining two notches with the shoulder seams. Evenly distribute and pin the rest of the neck band to the neckline, making sure it is not twisted. You'll notice the neck band is shorter than the neckline.

5 ATTACH THE NECK BAND

Starting from the seam at the back of the neck band, sew the neck band in place with a ⅜in (1cm) seam allowance and a zigzag stitch or an overlocker/serger. You'll need to stretch the neck band with your fingers as you sew to fit the neckline.

6 PRESS THE NECK BAND

Push the seam allowance downwards into the tank top and press the neck band up. Use a low heat setting on your iron and a pressing cloth to protect the fabric.

7 PREPARE THE ARM BANDS

Prepare the arm bands in the same way as the neck band (see step 3): match the ends, right sides together, and join them, unfold your ring of fabric and then refold lengthways with wrong sides together and cut or mark a notch opposite the seam – this will match to the shoulder seam of the tank. You don't need the other two notches at the quarter points this time.

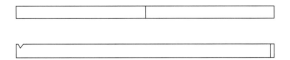

8 PIN ON THE ARM BANDS

Align the seam of each arm band to the side seam of the top (at the bottom of the armhole) with right sides and raw edges are together. Next, align the notch with the shoulder seam. Evenly distribute and pin the rest of the arm band to the armhole, making sure it is not twisted. You'll notice the arm band is shorter than the armhole.

9 ATTACH THE ARM BAND

Starting from the top back of the armhole, sew the arm band to the armhole with a ⅜in (1cm) seam allowance and a zigzag stitch or an overlocker/serger. You'll need to stretch the arm band with your fingers as you sew to fit the armhole. Repeat to attach the second arm band to the other armhole.

10 PRESS THE ARM BANDS

Push the seam allowances of the arm bands into the tank top and press the bands outwards. Use a low heat setting on your iron and a pressing cloth to protect the fabric.

11 SEW THE HEM

To finish, fold the bottom of your tank top to the wrong side by ⅜in (1cm) and press. Then fold the edge again, this time by 1in (2.5cm), and pin in place. Sew close to the edge using a zigzag stitch or twin needle on your sewing machine and press for a crisp finish.

BUTTON-FRONT DRESS

This button-front dress has a deep V-neck for a trendier take on a classic style. The lined bodice has darts to help you achieve the perfect fit around the bust but with a looser fit around the waist and hips for comfort. The skirt has stylish loops and shank buttons for a pretty closure that's easier to sew than you think! It makes for the perfect evening dress that moves beautifully in a drapey fabric.

DIFFICULTY LEVEL

Advanced

MATERIALS

- 3.65–4.4yd (3.3–4m) of 50in (127cm) wide woven fabric

- 0.9yd (0.8m) of 35in (89cm) wide lightweight woven interfacing

- 12 shank buttons ⅜in (1cm) wide

- A loop turner or turning set to turn out the button loops

FABRIC SUGGESTIONS

Light to medium-weight woven fabric such as cotton, linen, viscose or crepe.

THE PATTERNS

Print out the pdf at 100% scale and double-check that the square on the first page is 1in (2.5cm). There is also an A0 pattern that you can send off to be printed if you don't want to bother with sticking all the A4/US letter pages together.

SIZE CHART

Size	Bust	Waist	Hips
6	31in (79cm)	24in (61cm)	34in (86cm)
8	33in (84cm)	26in (66cm)	36in (91cm)
10	35in (89cm)	28in (71cm)	38in (96cm)
12	37in (94cm)	30in (76cm)	40in (101cm)
14	39in (99cm)	32in (81cm)	42in (106cm)
16	41in (104cm)	34in (86cm)	44in (111cm)
18	43in (109cm)	36in (91cm)	46in (116cm)
20	45in (114cm)	38in (96cm)	48in (121cm)
22	47in (119cm)	40in (101cm)	50in (126cm)
24	49in (124cm)	42in (106cm)	52in (132cm)
26	51in (129cm)	44in (111cm)	54in (137cm)
28	53in (134cm)	46in (116cm)	56in (142cm)
30	55in (139cm)	48in (121cm)	58in (147cm)
32	57in (144cm)	50in (126cm)	60in (152cm)

FINISHED GARMENT MEASUREMENTS

Size	Bust	Waist	Hips
6	31½in (80cm)	28in (71cm)	38in (96cm)
8	33½in (85cm)	30in (76cm)	40in (101cm)
10	35½in (90cm)	32in (81cm)	42in (106cm)
12	37½in (95cm)	34in (86cm)	44in (111cm)
14	39½in (100cm)	36in (91cm)	46in (116cm)
16	41½in (105cm)	38in (96cm)	48in (121cm)
18	43½in (110cm)	40in (101cm)	50in (126cm)
20	45½in (115cm)	42in (106cm)	52in (132cm)
22	47½in (120cm)	44in (111cm)	54in (137cm)
24	49½in (125cm)	46in (116cm)	56in (142cm)
26	51½in (130cm)	48in (121cm)	58in (147cm)
28	53½in (135cm)	50in (126cm)	60in (152cm)
30	55½in (140cm)	52in (132cm)	62in (157cm)
32	57½in (145cm)	54in (137cm)	64in (162cm)

PATTERN LAYOUTS

Refer to the pattern layouts for how to arrange the pattern pieces on your fabric, choosing the one that matches the width of fabric you have chosen. Cut out your pattern pieces.

FABRIC | SIZES 6–16 | 3.65 YD (3.3M)
FABRIC | SIZES 18–32 | 4.4 YD (4M)
Fabric width: 50in (127cm)

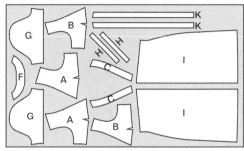

SINGLE LAYER OF FABRIC

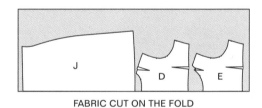

FABRIC CUT ON THE FOLD

INTERFACING | ALL SIZES | 0.9YD (0.8M)
Fabric width: 35in (88cm)

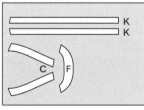

SINGLE LAYER OF FABRIC

1 FUSE ON THE INTERFACING

Fuse the interfacing onto the wrong side of the skirt
facings, front neck facings and back neck facing.

RIGHT SIDE
OF FABRIC

WRONG SIDE
OF FABRIC

2 MARK DARTS ON THE FABRIC

Use a water-soluble pen or chalk to draw the darts on
the wrong side of all the bodice pieces, including the
linings. (See page 58 for additional help with marking
and sewing darts.)

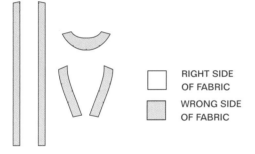

3 SEW THE DARTS

Fold the first dart to match up the long drawn lines, right sides together. Pin in place and sew, starting from the seam edge and stitching towards the tip of the dart. Leave a long thread tail at the tip of the dart, then tie a knot to secure the threads. Press the dart towards the centre. Repeat to sew all the remaining darts.

4 ATTACH THE BACK BODICE FACING

With right sides together, align the back bodice facing to the back bodice lining at the neckline. The bottom notches on the facing need to align with the top edge of the lining. Match the notches, then pin and sew using a $\frac{3}{8}$in (1cm) seam allowance. Clip the curves and press the seam upwards to create a smooth finish.

5 ATTACH THE FRONT BODICE FACING

With right sides together, align one front bodice facing to one front bodice lining at the neckline. Match the notches, then pin and sew with a $\frac{3}{8}$in (1cm) seam allowance. Press the seam allowances towards the facing. Repeat to attach the other front facing to the second front bodice lining piece.

6 JOIN THE BODICE LINING PIECES

Place the front bodice lining pieces right sides together with the back bodice lining and pin the side seams and shoulder seams. Sew, taking a $\frac{3}{8}$in (1cm) seam allowance, then press the seam allowances towards the back.

7 JOIN THE BODICE OUTER PIECES

Pin the front bodice pieces right sides together with the back bodice and then sew the side seams and shoulder seams, just as you did for the bodice lining. Press the seam allowances towards the back.

8 SEW THE NECKLINE

Pin the bodice and bodice lining right sides together, matching the shoulder seams and edges. Sew around the front and back neckline with a ⅜in (1cm) seam allowance. Before turning this out, press only the bodice lining make this gap between the two separate illustrations bigger as it looks confusing too close together hem pieces to the wrong side by ⅜in (1cm).

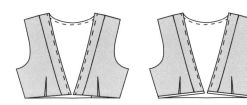

9 UNDERSTITCH THE NECKLINE

Turn the bodice right-side out. Press all the seams and understitch the front and back neckline (see page 17). To do this, open out your front bodice with the right side of the fabric facing you. Push the seam allowance of the neckline towards the facing and sew a line of stitching close to the edge of the neckline on the facing fabric so you stitch through the facing and the seam allowances underneath. Understitch around the front and back necklines, then roll the lining inside and press for a neat finish.

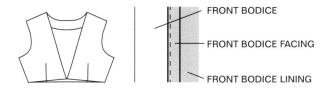

FRONT BODICE

FRONT BODICE FACING

FRONT BODICE LINING

10 SEW THE SKIRT SIDE SEAMS

Pin the front skirt pieces right sides together with the back skirt, with the side seam of each front skirt piece matching a side seam of the back skirt. Sew with a ⅜in (1cm) seam allowance. Finish the seams using an overlocker/serger, zigzag stitch or pinking shears, then press the seams towards the back.

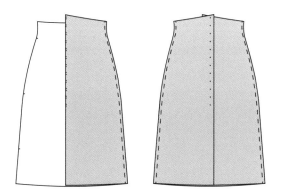

11 MAKE THE BUTTON LOOPS

Fold one button-loop piece in half lengthways with right sides together and pin. Sew along the length with a ⅜in (1cm) seam allowance. Repeat with the second button-loop piece then turn both pieces right-side out – a loop turner or turning set will make this easier.

Cut each strip into six 2in (5cm) button loops so you have twelve button loops in total. There will be excess, which you can put to one side.

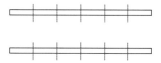

Use your fingers to ease each button loop into a U-shape and then use an iron to flatten and press each one so it holds its shape.

12 BASTE ON THE BUTTON LOOPS

Place the button loops on the right side of the right skirt front, as shown, aligning them at regular intervals using the notches provided. The first button loop will be just over ⅜in (1cm) below the waist of the skirt. Baste/tack these in place using a long stitch length and a ¼in (0.5cm) seam allowance.

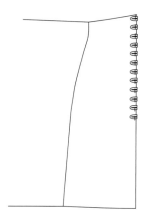

13 FINISH THE EDGES OF THE SKIRT FACINGS

On the skirt facing pieces, finish the outer raw edge – the side without the notch – starting from the top and then going down to the bottom edge and across it to finish the bottom edge as well. Use an overlocker/serger, zigzag stitch or pinking shears for this.

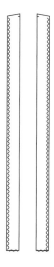

14 ATTACH THE FIRST SKIRT FACING

Pin the unfinished edge of a skirt facing right sides together with the front edge of the skirt front which has the button loops (the right front). The slightly tapered end of the facing should be at the top and the notches should match. Sew with a $\frac{3}{8}$in (1cm) seam allowance.

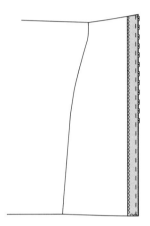

15 UNDERSTITCH THE SKIRT FACING

Flip the skirt facing to the right side and press the seam flat. Push the seam allowance of the skirt towards the facing and sew a line of stitching close to the seam on the facing fabric to understitch it. This will catch the seam allowances underneath the facing and keep them from moving. Continue down the entire length, then roll the facing to the inside and press for a neat finish.

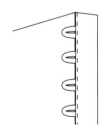 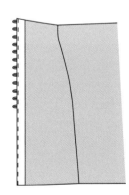

16 ATTACH THE SECOND SKIRT FACING

Repeat steps 14 and 15 to attach the second skirt facing to the left front skirt.

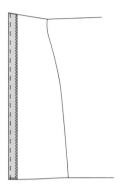

17 JOIN THE BODICE & SKIRT

Align the skirt with the waist edge of the bodice, right sides together, matching the beginning of the skirt facing with the neck edge of the front bodice facing and continuing along the rest of the skirt waist edge, pinning as you go. Match the side seams on the bodice to the side seams on the skirt, and make sure that the bodice lining is kept out of the way. Sew with a $\frac{3}{8}$in (1cm) seam allowance, then press the seam up.

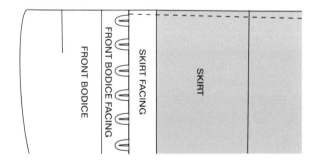

18 SEW THE BODICE LINING TO THE SKIRT

You should have already pressed the bottom of the bodice lining to the wrong side by ⅜in (1cm) towards the wrong side. If you missed this step, take the time to do it now. Arrange the pressed edge over the skirt waist seam to cover all the raw edges of the seam. With the lining just extending over the previous stitching line, pin along the entire waist. You can baste this in place before sewing. From the right side, sew a line of stitching in the existing waist seam to keep the bodice lining in place and create a neat finish. This is known as stitching in the ditch.

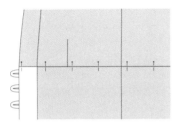

19 SEW GATHERING STITCH

Sew a gathering stitch ¼in (0.25cm) on the sleeve head across the notches. To do this, start by ensuring you have long thread tails at the start of your stitch and increase the stitch length to 4mm. Then sew a line of stiching across sleeve head. Don't backstitch at the beginning or end and leave long thread tails at the end. Repeat for the other sleeve.

20 SEW THE SLEEVE UNDERARM SEAMS

Fold each sleeve lengthways, with right sides together, and align and pin the underarm edges. Sew with a ⅜in (1cm) seam allowance then press the seam allowances towards the back.

21 HEM THE SLEEVES

Fold the bottom of each sleeve to the wrong side by ⅜in (1cm) and press. Fold the edge again, this time by ½in (1.2cm) and pin along the hem. Sew close to the edge and press for a crisp finish.

22 SEW IN THE SLEEVES

Treat the bodice lining and bodice as one when attaching the sleeves. First, open out each sleeve and gently pull the gathering stitch around the top to create a few ripples in the fabric – use your fingers to even them out. With the bodice wrong-side out and the sleeve right-side out, insert the sleeve inside the bodice so the two are right sides together. Align the top of the sleeve head with the shoulder seam and match the front and back notches together. Gently adjust the gathering stitch to help ease in the sleeve head between the notches. Pin and sew the sleeve to the armhole with a $\frac{3}{8}$in (1cm) seam allowance. Finish the seam in your preferred way. Repeat to attach the other sleeve.

24 ATTACH THE BUTTONS

Lay out the dress, with the front right-side up, and line up the centre-front skirt pieces so the button loops overlap the skirt. Mark the button placement by taking chalk or a water-soluble pen and making a dot through the button loop onto the skirt. You can also use the button guides on the pattern piece. You'll want to mark the button placement at the end of each loop, so it has tension to keep it from popping open. Sew on the twelve $\frac{3}{8}$in (1cm) shank buttons and fasten the loops to finish.

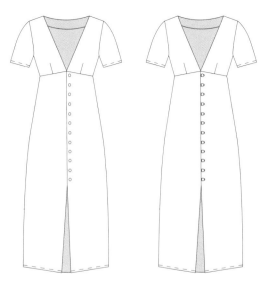

23 HEM THE SKIRT

For a neat finish, first sew the skirt facing to the skirt along the bottom edges with right sides together and using a $\frac{3}{4}$in (2cm) seam allowance. Stop at the edge of the facing. Turn the facing right-side out and use your fingers to make the edge look defined and sharp. Repeat on the other facing and press the edges in place. Finally, press the remaining skirt hem to the wrong side by $\frac{3}{4}$in (2cm) and sew in place.

INDEX

adjusting patterns 27
    full-bust adjustments 28–31
    lengthening and shortening 27
    small-bust adjustment 31

backstitching 14
bags
    Tie Tote Bag 69–73
    Trendy Tote Bag 83–4
basting 14
binding 14
bodices 14
buttons 44–5
    Button-back Top 105–11
    Button-front Dress 52, 177–87
    stitching options 44

Camisole Dress and Top 56, 97–102
clipping 14
clips 11, 15
Cover-up and Summer Jacket 131–7
Cut-out Dress 139–47
cutting mats 13

darts 14, 22
    sewing darts 58–9
digital patterns 24
    assembling pattern pages 25
    printing pattern 25
    QR code 9
Drawstring Trousers and Shorts 157–65
dresses
    Button-front Dress 52, 177–87
    Camisole Dress and Top 56, 97–102
    Cut-out Dress 139–47
    Halter-neck Dress and Top 56, 113–17
    Shirred Dress and Top 52, 87–95

ease 14
equipment 10–13

fabrics 18
    buying swatches 19
    challenging fabrics 19
    cutting 35
    drape 14
    fabric markers 13
    right and wrong sides 17
    selvedges/selvages 17
    stretch fabrics 19
    woven fabrics 18
facing 15

gathering 15, 52–3
grading patterns 15, 26

Halter-neck Dress and Top 56, 113–17
hems 15
    double-fold hems 38
    single-fold hems 38
    twin-needle hems 38

interfacing 15
ironing 11, 43

jacket
    Cover-up and Summer Jacket 131–7

lining 15
loop turners 13

Maxi Skirt 75–81
measurements 20
    finished garment measurements 21
    length adjustments 21

needles 10, 13

overlockers 13, 40

patterns 15, 22
    basic pattern adjustments 27–31
    cutting lines 22
    darts 14, 22
    digital patterns 9, 24–5
    fold lines 23
    grainlines 15, 22
    how to grade a pattern 15, 26
    key 23
    lengthening and shortening lines 22
    notches 15, 22
    pattern weights 13
    tracing 23
pinking shears 13, 40
pins 11, 15
pockets 46–9

rotary cutters 13
rulers 11

safety pins 11
scissors 10
Scrunchie 65–6
seams 17
    common sewing problems 43
    finishing 15, 40–1
    French seams 41
    grading 15
    seam allowance 17
    seam rippers 11
    sewing knit fabrics 38, 43
    sewing woven fabrics 38
selvedges/selvages 17
sergers 13, 40
sewing 7–9
    failed projects 32
    glossary of terms 14–17
sewing machines 10
    needles 10, 43
shirring 50–1
    Shirred Dress and Top 52, 87–95
shorts
    Drawstring Trousers and Shorts 157–65
side slits 60–1

size charts 17
skirts
    Maxi Skirt 75–81
    Stretch Midi Skirt 149–53
staystitching 17
stitching in the ditch 17
straps 56–7
stretch fabrics 19
    attaching knit binding/bands 54–5
    Stretch Midi Skirt 149–53

tacking 14
tailor's clappers 13
Tammy Handmade 7, 190
Tank Top 54, 169–75
tape measures 11
techniques 37
    how to attach knit binding/bands 54–5
    how to gather fabric 52–3
    how to shirr fabric 50–1
    pockets 46–9
    seams 38–43
    sewing darts 58–9
    sewing on buttons 44–5
    sewing side slits 60–1
    sewing skinny straps 56–7
thread 10, 43
Tie Tote Bag 69–73
Tie-front Top 52, 121–9
toiles 17
tools 10–13
tops
    Button-back Top 105–11
    Camisole Dress and Top 56, 97–102
    Halter-neck Dress and Top 56, 113–17
    Shirred Dress and Top 52, 87–95
    Tank Top 54, 169–75
    Tie-front Top 52, 121–9
topstitching 17
Trendy Tote Bag 83–4
trousers
    Drawstring Trousers and Shorts 157–65
turning sets 13

understitching 17

zigzag stitching 40

ABOUT THE AUTHOR

Tammy Johal is a sewing pattern designer and content creator based in the UK. Her stylish pattern brand Tammy Handmade has been sewn and loved by thousands of sewists across the world. She has built a large and successful online community through social media where she shares sewing and pattern-making inspiration that encourages others to learn. Formerly a graphic designer, Tammy now spends her time crafting easy-to-follow sewing patterns and working with global craft brands to create engaging social content.

FIND TAMMY HERE:

Instagram: @tammy.handmade
TikTok: @tammy.handmade
Youtube: @tammy.handmade
Website: www.tammyhandmade.com

Show us what you made with this book by using the hashtag #SewSimpleBook and tagging me on Instagram!

ACKNOWLEDGEMENTS

If someone told me at the start of my sewing journey that I'd one day write my own book, I would have laughed! I can't believe that something that started as a hobby, from sewing in the corner of my bedroom, has blossomed into a skill that's changed my life. Learning to sew has been a truly transformative experience and I want to thank all the incredible people that have helped me get to where I am now.

Thank you to such a supportive sewing community, for always believing in me and helping turn my passion into so much more. I love being a part of an online space that connects us all with our love for sewing and inspires us to create every day. Thank you to all my Tammy Handmade Makers for purchasing my sewing patterns and following along my journey as I grow and continue to create easy-to-follow patterns for you. It's always been my mission and what fuels my creativity.

Thank you to my partner, Kieran. Working on pinch-me projects like this book can feel very daunting and overwhelming at times, but I'm so thankful I've always had you by my side to support me at every step. You always manage to pick me up when I need extra motivation and I can't imagine navigating this world without you.

Thank you to the wonderful team at Quadrille. To my editor Harriet and designer Alicia, I can't thank you enough for helping me bring this book to life and encouraging me every step of the way to keep creating and doing what I love. Writing this book has been an incredible experience and I couldn't have done this without you two.

Thank you to all my family and friends for your constant love and support for everything I do in life. To my mum Anita, my Nani Surjit, my Massi Arpana and my Mammi Raj, you have always been the biggest cheerleaders I could ask for and I am so fortunate to have such supportive women in my family. To my friends Leona, Jessica and Hayley, thank you for your patience and always finding a way to make me laugh when I need it most. I wouldn't be where I am today without the love and support from you all.

Quadrille, Penguin Random House UK, One Embassy Gardens, 8 Viaduct Gardens, London SW11 7BW

Quadrille Publishing Limited is part of the Penguin Random House group of companies whose addresses can be found at global.penguinrandomhouse.com

Penguin
Random House
UK

Published by Quadrille in 2025
www.penguin.co.uk

A CIP catalogue record for this book is available from the British Library

ISBN 978 183 783 303 0
10 9 8 7 6 5 4 3 2 1

Managing Director Sarah Lavelle
Editorial Director Harriet Butt
Design and Art Direction Alicia House
Photographer Emily Lavarello
Props Stylist Harriet Langsbury
Make Up Artist Laura Adkins and Helen Lancaster
Models Elena Forrest, Tammy Johal and Nina Uhl
Grading Grade House Ltd
Makers Katya Yurova and Susan Young
Production Director Stephen Lang
Production Controller Sumayyah Waheed

Colour reproduction by F1

Printed in China by C&C Offset Printing Co., Ltd.

The authorised representative in the EEA is Penguin Random House Ireland, Morrison Chambers, 32 Nassau Street, Dublin D02 YH68.

Penguin Random House is committed to a sustainable future for our business, our readers and our planet. This book is made from Forest Stewardship Council® certified paper.

MIX
Paper | Supporting
responsible forestry
FSC® C018179